Wayne Moore's

Fly Tying Notes

Recreation Consultants, Seattle, WA

Dedicated to Catherine, Peggy and Bill

Wayne Moore's
Fly Tying Notes
is published by
Recreation Consultants
P.O. Box 842
Seattle, Washington 98111

First Printing, November 1984

Artwork by Wayne Moore
Photographs by Catherine Moore.

INTRODUCTION

I have been called a perfectionist many times. I confess that I do not know what this means.

With fly tying, as with most things in life, a little extra effort produces better results. I welcome the title "perfectionist" if it means that I will not make excuses for mediocrity or sloppy work.

Some people feel that salmon flies are the epitome of the fly tyer's art. I disagree.

Although highly colorful and elaborate (some salmon flies require 36 different feathers), a salmon fly's symmetry and shape can make it awkward looking.

To me a sparsely dressed fly is every bit as beautiful and significant to the fly tyer's art as a garish salmon fly. A properly tied wooly worm, a Cahill, muddler minnow or squirrel hair nymph, when tied with precision and care, is as fine a work of art as you will ever see.

I am convinced that tying better flies takes a bit more effort. But a better end product—flies that are pleasing to both man and fish—will be the result. If that is what perfectionists strive for, then I am certainly one.

It is with this in mind that I have yielded to requests from fly fishermen and fly tyers I have met over the years and gathered my bits and pieces together in one book. My ideas and techniques have evolved from many sources during more than a half century of effort. Most of them have not appeared in any other resource. They have, however, been part of the Bulletin of the White River Fly Fishers in Mountain Home, Arkansas.

I hope that my collection of notes will be helpful to other fly tyers. My innovations such as the Wayne Moore Bobbin, which I originally designed in the 1940's, have developed over many years and I have refined them constantly. Some of my ideas have been imitated by others; however, my *original* designs are presented here and I will be pleased if you find them useful.

By utilizing some of the tools and ideas described in this book, I hope you will find that fly tying will become easier, more enjoyable and your end product—the flies—will be of better, more uniform quality.

Wayne E. Moore
April, 1984
Mountain Home, Arkansas

ABOUT THE AUTHOR

Born and raised in the southern United States, Wayne Moore started tying flies as a youngster. He lived and worked for 40 years in Wisconsin as a research chemist in wood and wood products.

During his lifetime Wayne fished many areas of the U.S. and caught most species of fish, including musky, on a fly rod. He also fished the Miramichi in New Brunswick and the River Spey in Scotland for salmon.

He taught many people to tie flies and fly fish. He enjoyed helping others and was well known for his teaching proficiency.

The White River Fly Fishers grew to an enthusiastic membership of 200 while Wayne was President of the club for two years. He was active in conservation projects and for eight years he was involved in planting trout eggs in the White River system with the Whitlock-Vibert Box.

In 1981 he received the Award of Excellence from the Midwest Council of the Federation of Fly Fishers. He served as chairman of the Midwest Conclave and as chairman of fly tyers at midwest conclaves. He was Vice President of the Southern Council of F.F.F. for two years. He attended 13 local and national conclaves where he took part in fly tying demonstrations and activities. He was chairman of the fly tyers at the National F.F.F. Conclave at West Yellowstone, Montana. He served as a director of the Federation of Fly Fishers for two years. Moore received the Man of the Year Award from the White River Fly Fishers in 1984.

Wayne died April 17, 1984 unexpectedly at the age of 70. He had just completed the manuscript for this book.

TABLE OF CONTENTS

CLEAN HOOK EYES

Few things are more irritating than trying to thread a leader through a hook eye clogged with head cement. This is so unnecessary. To avoid a cement-clogged hook eye, prepare a hackle feather by stripping the fluff near the base of the feather for about 1/2 inch. If head cement accidentally gets into the hook eye, pass the stem of the hackle through the eye so that the hackle fibers absorb the excess cement before it dries. A clean hook eye will be the result.

WASHING MATERIALS

It is a good idea to wash all natural necks, feathers, fur, and hair or skins as they are received. Use a mild kitchen detergent. You will be amazed at the amount of dirt that is removed. Thorough washing will also remove larvae and insect eggs. Dry the fur or hair on a clothes line in the shade. A hot sun may cause fat to melt and run. Necks can be alternately hung on a clothes line and placed between paper towels and newspapers. A light board placed on top of newspapers will keep the neck skins flat. Feathers and hair will straighten out, be brighter in color, and more pleasant to use. Dyed materials have usually been well washed and may not need cleaning.

LEGS ON INSECT-TYPE WET FLIES

For many years fly tyers have wound a collar of hackle at the front of a wet fly. The hackle on top is pulled underneath the hook where tying thread holds the feathers in position. The hackles slant down and to the rear. In another method, a beard of hackle is tied on the underside of the hook at the front of the fly. Both methods cause legs (hackle) to originate from the head or front of the fly.

Insect legs are spread out along the body in the area of the thorax—not the head.

Try this: Dub a tapered fur body from the bend of the hook to a little more than 1/2 the length of the hook shank. Tie off dubbing and tie in hackle. Wind more dubbing, to form thorax, up to head area. Then wind hackle for legs through the thorax. Tie off hackle and trim it off the top of the hook. Tie in the wing and form a neat head. The legs will be spread out along the body and come from a more central part of the simulated insect. Try using this method on a small wet Cahill, and you'll be pleasantly surprised at the result.

HARD BODIED ANTS

Trout seem to like ants for the formic acid that they contain (the family name for ants is Formicidae). Ants are the most numerous of all insects in America and can vary in length from a full inch to 1/16 inch. A size 16 (9671) hook is a good starting choice for the following fly.

Use acetate floss to form a hump, similar to the abdomen (gaster) of an ant, on the rear 1/3 of the hook. Wind tying thread forward to form peticel or waist of ant. Tie in hackle and wind about two turns at the front of the peticel. Use acetate floss to form a smaller ball for the head between hackle and eye of hook. Whip finish and dip fly in acetone or ethyl-acetate for 30 seconds. Remove and shake to remove excess solvent. The acetate floss will partially dissolve and stay in place, and upon removal from the solvent it will harden into a smooth body that is practically indestructible. The solvent will not affect the feather hackle. Good colors are all black with black hackle and rusty-reddish-brown with brown hackle. A small humped (kinked) shank popper hook makes an attractive ant.

STORAGE OF TYING MATERIALS

After washing and drying, place all fur and feathers (from whatever source) in an isolation jar containing paradichlorobenzene for a week to ten days before adding new material to your other supplies. A wide mouth gallon jar with a tight top is ideal. Pickle, mustard, or mayonnaise jars can be obtained from restaurants or delicatessens for about 25 cents each. After the isolation stage, store materials in tight containers with paradichlorobenzene moth balls. Premium cracker cans (Nabisco) are square 4-1/2" x 4-1/2" x 9-1/2" tall. Because of their shape a number of necks may be stored in each can. I store each neck in a heavy paper open-end envelope with an ink blotter or soft cardboard next to the skin to absorb fat or grease. Suitable envelopes can be made from buff letter files (.010" thick) or open-end legal envelopes (11F, Smead Co.) may be purchased at office supply stores.

MIXED COLORS FOR FLIES

I have never seen an insect, nymph, minnow, or crustacean that is one solid color. These important trout foods have spots, areas, or hairs of different colors that blend to give an overall effect. This effect will vary with light and water conditions. It stands to reason that the most effective flies are made from mixtures of colors. Hackles, bodies, wings, legs, and tails can be made from blends of several spectrum colors and shades. Hair wings can be readily blended in a tube type "stacker." I use stackers (hair eveners) made from streamline copper water pipe with a cap on the bottom. A stacker made from 7/8" outer dimension pipe is handy for blending hair wings. Drop different color hair into the stacker with the fine or pointed end of the hair down. To mix, stir with a small stirring rod. Tap the stacker to even the ends of the hair and you have a mixed color wing for either streamers or winged insects.

WET METHOD
Blending of Hair, Fur,
and Synthetic Materials for Dubbing

Among the several methods for blending fur, the most widely used are the wet and dry methods.

Blending fur by the wet method: Place clipped furs (1/2-3/4" long) in a pan of warm water containing a small amount of soap. Stir to mix well and pour through a screen-type strainer or a piece of fine screen wire. Wash free of soap in running water. Remove mat of fur and dry. The felted mass should be well blended and makes excellent dubbing. (By the way, a modification of this method, where the fur is deposited on a dome, is used to make fur hats.)

DRY METHOD
Blending of Fur and Synthetic Yarns

You may purchase a "mini-blender" from fly tying supply shops. This is actually a small coffee grinder. Most of the ones that I have seen are made in Italy and cost $15 to $20. They work reasonably well for small amounts of mixed material.

A better deal is a "Waring type" kitchen blender. If you have a blender of this type, purchase an extra head and jars used to prepare baby foods from the manufacturer's service center. These jars will handle about 1/2 pint of material. The head is made of plastic, contains the blades, and screws onto the jar much like a fruit jar cap. The cost is less than half the cost of the "mini-blender" and is much more satisfactory. By purchasing the extra head you will keep peace in the family by not getting hair in mixed food preparations. You will have variable speeds, much more power and better mixing.

If the fur sticks to the sides of the jar, or balls up and refuses to mix, you probably have static electricity problems. This may happen when fur is very dry. If you have static charge problems, spray a tissue lightly with "Static Guard" (Alberto-Culver Co.). Wipe the jar with the sprayed tissue. It works wonders by keeping individual hair strands separated during blending operations.

BLENDING SYNTHETICS

Synthetic yarns such as "Kodel" polyester (Aunt Lydia's rug yarn), orlon, acrylic, sparkle yarn (acrylic plus a special type of nylon), "Frostlon," "Mohlon" and many others make excellent fly bodies, especially for wet flies and nymphs. Cut yarn in varying lengths of 1/2" to 3/4" and place in blender. The yarn will disintegrate into individual fibers and look like a fluffy ball of fine fur that is easy to dub. Skeins of Coats and Clark "Persian type" acrylic needlepoint and crewel yarn can be bought at Wal-Mart for 25 cents each. A nice gray can be made as follows:

Color of Yarn	Yellow	Red	Blue	White
Color Number	457	810	742	1
Length Used	12"	4"	8"	36"

Store in a bottle with the above label so that the color can be reproduced as wanted.

A mixture that matches fox squirrel belly is made as follows:

Color of Yarn	Light Tan	Burnt Orange
Color Number	492	416
Length Used	30"	12"

Use care when blending Kodel because matting can damage a blender. This can be prevented by using smaller portions or by adding a small amount of neutral color fur.

MIXED HACKLES

Mixed hackles are very effective as they nearly match the color and light reflection patterns of real insects. The Adams dry fly is very effective and is perhaps the most widely sold dry fly. This popular fly is hackled with a mixture of grizzly and brown. If you do not have good grizzly hackles, try dark dun gray, white or cream, and brown. Variant or cree feathers are flecked and are usually of good quality. Try mixing them with medium dun gray.

Dun gray flies can be hackled with two shades of gray to give a life-like appearance.

Light cahills may be improved by using two shades of cream or light ginger.

Medium brown or medium ginger hackles mixed with cream hackles results in effective light ginger.

Mixtures of red and yellow saddle hackles on yellow bass poppers have always been good fish getters.

Use your ingenuity. Try flies of mixed colors and hackles. You may save money by not having to use the most expensive necks.

RUSTY NYMPH

The following fly has been most effective. Many large rainbow trout have been caught with this fly in various parts of the country, by different fly fishermen.

Hook: size 12, mustad 9671.

Thread: brown, Herb Howard 6/0.

Weighted: lead wire .016″ or 1 amp. fuse wire.

Tail: Ringneck pheasant tail fibers.

Abdomen: Aunt Lydia's Kodel polyester rug yarn. Rust color No. 325. Cut into 1/2″ to 3/4″ lengths and blend for dubbing. This yarn has more luster, is more translucent, and is more "brownish" than Fly Rite rust.

Rib: copper wire B and S No. 36, .005″ diameter.

Thorax: same as abdomen.

Hackle: Variant, cree or feather that will give speckled legs.

Wing Case: Peacock herl.

1. Wind thread on fore part of hook—beginning 1/8″ or 2 mm from eye and continue for about 5/32″, 4 mm or a little less than half of a hook shank. Soak with head cement.
2. Wind lead wire for about nine or ten turns over thread base. Wind thread at ends of lead wire to hold it in place and apply cement.
3. Wind thread toward rear of hook. Tie in copper wire and wind thread to point above the barb of the hook.
4. Tie in about five fibers from center tail feather of ringneck pheasant so that tail will extend to rear about 9/32″ or 7 mm.

5. Dub a tapered and rather small abdomen in a clockwise direction up to the rear of the lead winds. Abdomen will be about 1/4"-plus, or 6 mm long. Fuzz up abdomen if necessary.
6. Rib copper wire in opposite direction (counterclockwise) about five turns and tie off at rear of lead winds.
7. Tie in about seven strands of peacock herl on top of hook at rear of lead wire.
8. Tie in hackle at rear of thorax area.
9. Dub thorax area heavier than abdomen for about 5/32", or 4 mm—leave about 1/16" for head.
10. Wind about three turns of hackle forward through thorax area and tie off. Cut off excess hackle.
11. Divide hackle on top and push to sides of fly.
12. Pull peacock herl forward, tie down, and trim. Wind a small head. Whip finish and apply two coats of head cement.

WEIGHTED FLY BODIES

Wind lead wire approximately the same size as hook shank on the front one third of the hook. This will make the finished fly ride better in the water. Leave enough room next to the hook eye for wings, hackle, and a small head. Too much lead will cause the hook to turn over and ride upside down. In such a case, construct the fly upside down. A fly tied in the conventional way, going down river upside down, does not look very natural, to say the least.

If possible wind lead wire over a cement-soaked thread base. Wind thread tightly at ends of lead and taper thread to level of lead. This will prevent turning or sliding of lead on the hook. Thread wound over lead does little or nothing to prevent movement of the lead. Coat lead with head cement or epoxy to add strength and to prevent discoloration of body materials by the corroding lead.

For flat bodied flies, the lead windings may be flattened with pliers. Too much flattening causes the lead to crumble into small pieces. For a more substantial flat body, wind oversized lead wire along each side of the hook with thread, and cement with epoxy cement. Do a dozen at a time for maximum efficiency.

FLOSS BODIES

Many times, when winding rayon or nylon floss, static charges cause the ends of the fibrils, which make up the floss, to stick up. These fiber ends hang up and stick to everything to cause rough uneven bodies. Moisten the floss a little and pull through your fingers. This will remove the static charge and will make a smooth and even fly body. For small flies, a nice taper is obtained when the floss is tied in near the front, wound to the rear and back to the front. This avoids the hump that is present when floss is tied in at the rear of the hook. For large flies build a tapered under-body with padding cotton string or with a strip of art foam or curon of a color that matches the floss. When your fingers are rough or when you are tying large flies, a bobbin for the floss is helpful and will prevent soiling or discoloration of the floss.

GUARD HAIRS

For small midges and flies (size 16 to 18) it is usually better to use underfur, with guard hairs removed, for dubbing. The guard hairs are longer and much stiffer than the underfur. To remove guard hairs, cut fur close to skin. Grasp fur at cut end (skin end) with left thumb and finger, and pluck or pull guard hairs out with right thumb and fingers.

Don't discard the guard hairs just because they don't fit in the small fly. On some patterns, such as hare's ear, sow bug, scud and shrimp, guard hairs should remain in the fur to give a rough, shaggy appearance.

For some patterns, such as shrimp or scuds, it is helpful if you add extra guard hairs to form the legs. Use the guard hairs saved from the small flies above to enrich the guard hair content of your dubbing for patterns that need them. Mix underfur and guard hairs thoroughly in blender. In some cases, I add guard hairs from some other type of fur, such as mink of the proper color, to a fur that is short on guard hairs. Bottles containing dubbing can be labeled as follows: (1) guard hairs removed, (2) with guard hairs, or (3) extra guard hairs added.

HACKLE PROBLEMS

Many people have told me that sometimes they have difficulty with hackle feathers that will not stand up straight when wound on the hook. The fibers of the feather lay down more or less parallel to the hook shank. The problem may be related to the maturity of the feather.

Hackles taken from chickens at ages 9 and 10 months are as good as the feather will ever be. The quality of the feathers taken from roosters 2 to 3 years old will not improve but may have thicker and stiffer center ribs. This may cause considerable difficulty when winding on the fly. Some feathers may have an elongated oval and flattened center stem. Such a stem is shown in figure 1, section AA1. This can be due to genetics or age of the bird. Also, immature feathers may shrink to this configuration upon drying. It is best to avoid such feathers. If you strip more fibers from the base to a point higher upon the feather, you may find a center stem that is more like figure 1, section AA2. These small round center stems will stand on edge and wind much better. Look for necks that have small round center stems.

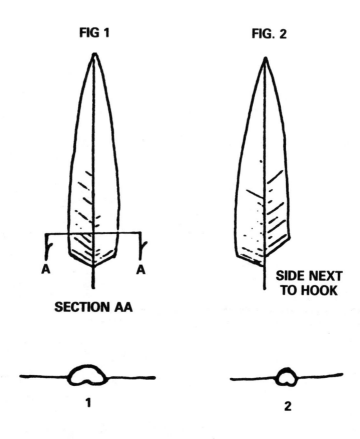

FIG 1

FIG. 2

SECTION AA

SIDE NEXT
TO HOOK

1

2

In some cases, problem feathers tied in at the tip instead of at the base will produce a better fly. This is done with saddle hackle on a wooly worm so as to form a tapered hackle, higher at the front of the fly. When tied in at the base of the feather, removing extra fibers from the side of the feather that will be next to the hook, as shown in figure 2, may be helpful in forming erect hackles on the hook. Using the thumb to crimp or flatten the stem of the feather, where it is tied in, can make the feather start to wind properly. Winding the first few turns with the fingers before attaching the hackle pliers leads to much better control of the hackle. When tying in the base end of a feather, tie underneath the hook and at an angle of about 45 degrees with the hook shank.

DUBBED FLY BODIES

There are dozens of methods for dubbing fur bodies which cannot be described in a short note. Some methods produce tightly wound segmented bodies; others are more loosely wound. Strive to wind a loose body that is durable. The loosely wound body will float longer than the tight body. Try it with polypropylene such as "Fly-Rite." Although polypropylene does not absorb water, the tight body will sink more quickly than the loose body. The loosely dubbed body will look more like an insect in water. In general good natural fur bodies float better than "Fly-Rite" bodies. The loosely dubbed body will trap lots of small air bubbles much as insects do in water. If a segmented body is called for, rib in the opposite direction with fine wire, tinsel, or transparent nylon thread.

CEMENTS FOR TIGHT BUCKTAIL OR HAIR STREAMER HEADS

Many commonly used head cements contain 15 percent or less solids and 85 percent solvent. They are not good adhesives when the butts of a bucktail fly are saturated with such cements and tightly wound. The hair may actually loosen when the space occupied by the solvent is left void as the solvent evaporates, and hairs will pull out.

Polyurethane varnish contains up to 45 percent solids and sets chemically. Fly heads saturated with polyurethane and wound tightly with tying thread will be practically indestructible. As the varnish squeezes out during the winding operation, absorb excess on a cloth. Allow to dry overnight and recoat with varnish applied with a dubbing needle. A very hard and durable head will be obtained. I have never had hair pull out of such flies even when used for fish that are tough on flies.

Pliobond is a good adhesive and remains flexible. Solids content is higher than most head cements; however, I do not like the toxicity of the solvent that is used in Pliobond.

Epoxy cements are good adhesives with high solids content. They set chemically and will produce strong, durable heads. It is difficult to use for fly tying because the cement should not be allowed to come in contact with fingers. Apply to head when the fly is finished.

PALMER HACKLED FLIES

For a more durable palmer hackled fly such as a wooly worm, wind a turn or two of the body material (chenille or dubbed fur) forward and let hang on hackle pliers. Tie in hackle, wind body material to forward position and then wind hackle forward through the body material. The stem of the hackle feather will be imbedded in the body and will be protected at the rear. If the hackle is tied in at the very rear of the body, it will sometimes slip down the bend of the hook. Fish teeth can also break the unprotected center stem of the hackle and cause the feather to unwind. I find that wooly worms tied as outlined above last many times longer.

CURVED FEATHERS

Feathers are used for wide tails and wings on streamers, matukas and sculpins. Normal practice is to place the concave sides of adjacent feathers together. This causes opposing curvatures of feathers to form a more or less straight wing. Feathers used are neck hackles, saddle hackles, hen neck feathers, and body feathers. Sometimes these feathers have exaggerated curvatures. When two to four feathers are used, this curvature is most troublesome because the feathers tend to twist and turn and resist staying in place.

The feathers can be straightened as follows: Place feathers in lukewarm water for a few minutes until soft. Place wet feather, curved side down, on a flat glass or lucite plate. Stretch and push the feather flat. The feather will stick to the plate. Allow to dry. The feather will be straight and will fluff out when handled. These straight feathers are easily tied in. The still slightly concave surfaces on opposing feathers are placed together to produce a matched and balanced wing or tail.

USE OF TINSEL

Many fly patterns call for a tinsel tag at the rear of the fly. Oval tinsel is most often used. Instead of tying in tinsel and winding tinsel to the rear and then forward, try this method of tying: Wind thread over tinsel, parallel with hook, to rear-most position of tag. Then wind thread forward and wind tinsel forward and tie off. Apply cement to tag and it will stay in place. Metallic tinsel on spools will be less likely to tarnish if stored in screw top bottles. This prevents fumes from the air coming in contact with the metal. A small piece of camphor placed in the bottle will also be effective. In my experience mylar tinsels stretch and are easily torn loose by fish. The French (Henri Verdura, tarnish proof) metallic tinsels are much more durable.

TINSEL BODIES

Long and smooth tinsel bodies for flies such as "Mickey Finn" may be made as follows:

Use medium width flat or embossed Henri Vendura metallic tinsel. For a silver body, use white tying thread. Tie in oval tinsel at the rear of the hook for rib. Wind thread to front of hook and tie in white floss (silk preferred). Wind floss tight and smooth to rear and then forward to front part of hook. Bind end of floss with tying thread and trim excess floss. Cut a taper about 3/8-inch long on end of tinsel. Tie in tapered end of tinsel. Wind tightly to rear and then forward and tie off. Do not let edges of tinsel overlap; instead wrap firmly edge to edge. Keep body flat; do not attempt a fat tapered body. (For a tapered body, use braided mylar tubing.) The white floss underbody will permit winding of a smoother tinsel body and will not show readily when winding errors are made. Wind oval tinsel rib forward and tie off. Apply two to three coats of head cement, clear lacquer or one coat of epoxy cement. For gold bodies, use gold floss underbody. Tinsel bodies made this way reflect lots of light, are good fish takers, and are durable.

SPARKLING YARN
Dazzle, Twinkle, Puff, Antron, Creslan, Kodel Polyester, Acrilon, Star Mist, Cruise

These are all names of relatively new yarns. For the most part they have been developed as rug yarns and are sold in stores as knitting yarns. These yarns sparkle in the light and collect air bubbles in the water similar to some insects. Six of the above yarns contain DuPont antron trilobal nylon. This is a nylon fiber triangular in cross section, flat on the sides, and twisting. It is coated with a permanent anti-static agent which helps prevent soiling and matting in a rug. This coating material causes the fibers to attract air bubbles in the water. The flat surfaces attract bubbles better than round fibers and tend to trap bubbles. In the laboratory the light reflection patterns of bubbles on insects and from trilobal nylon are almost identical. Because it does not mat or cling to itself, it holds its shape in water instead of soaking into a soggy mass of more or less parallel fibers. Since the material does not mat, the yarn can be cut into pieces, disintegrated and blended easily in a Waring type blender.

As purchased in the stores, antron fibers are blended with orlon or acrylic fibers: 60 percent acrylic/40 percent antron nylon. The antron fibers are clear while the acrylic is colored. This makes a very effective dubbing material. Sparkling yarn and puff are sold by Coats and Clark under the Red Heart label. They both contain 60 percent acrylic and 40 percent antron. The puff has a different twist to make it fluffy. It blends better than the sparkle yarn in mechanical blenders. Cruise, Unger French-made yarn, also sparkles and contains antron nylon fibers. Antron is the key word to look for on the yarn label.

Creslan is an orlon acrylic product by American Cyanamide made for rugs. Its sparkle is similar to antron-containing yarn. It does not mat. Acrilon is a bright acrylic yarn made by Monsanto. It does not trap air bubbles.

Kodel polyester (Aunt Lydia's rug yarn) sold by the American Thread Company, is a useful fly tying material. It has less sparkle than the other sparkle yarns and is not translucent (a characteristic of many insect bodies). It has been effectively used for nymph bodies for some time. It mats and tangles badly and is difficult to blend in a blender. Small portions must be used in order to avoid ruining the blender. Kodel is used in Jorgensen's "Seal-Ex" dubbing which is used as a replacement for now unavailable seal fur.

The yarns mentioned above are used in various blends of prepared dubbing materials sold in fly tying supply shops. Take your pick and have fun!

THE EYES HAVE IT

Minnows, tadpoles, frogs and many other water creatures have prominent and conspicuous eyes. Insects such as dragonflies, damsel flies, bees, water boatmen, house flies and many others have large eyes. Artificial fishing flies tied to simulate these are more effective with eyes. Streamers, deer hair flies, bass bug poppers, frogs, crayfish and shrimp can be fitted with durable eyes.

Many years ago we used glass taxidermist eyes formed on small iron wires. These wires were bent and tied on each side of the hook shank. Herters supplied thousands of these glass eyes. They were fragile and broke easily when hitting rocks, etc. Bead chain eyes are made by cutting two beads from the chain with the connecting link holding the two eyes together. They are tied on the hook and painted. They do not hold paint well. They are heavy and have sharp edges and holes for the pupils of the eyes. For small eyes, nylon leader material can be held near a flame source of heat so as to form balls on each end of the nylon.

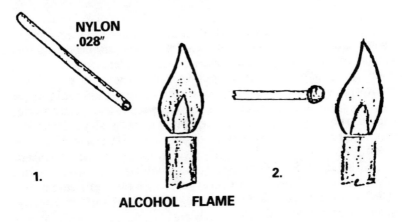

NYLON .028"

1.　　　　**2.**

ALCOHOL　FLAME

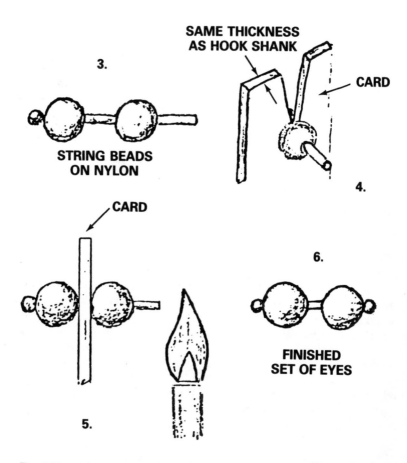

3.

STRING BEADS ON NYLON

SAME THICKNESS AS HOOK SHANK

CARD

4.

CARD

6.

FINISHED SET OF EYES

5.

By following steps 1 through 6 in the sketches above, you can make bead eyes that are durable. The beads are hard plastic and are usually made overseas and come in millimeter sizes; 2 mm to 4 mm are good sizes for most applications. They come in many colors; white, yellow and red are good colors for the iris part of the eye. The nylon can be dyed black or red for the pupil of the eye. The nylon should be held near the flame, not in it. The notched card provides proper spacing between the eyes so that they will fit the hook shank. They are tied on the hook with figure 8 wraps (about six wraps) and cemented in place. The body or head material will reinforce and cover part of the bead to form an eye that looks like an eye. This is a relatively easy operation and makes a nice looking and effective streamer or minnow simulator.

PAINTED EYES

Painted eyes can be easily and quickly applied to cork or balsa wood poppers and to streamer heads. I use smooth hardwood dowels that are flat on the ends and tapered to differing diameters. I have used the same sticks for over 40 years. Some people use nail heads but nail heads are rarely round, flat, and smooth. Nor do they hold paint very well. The sketches show typical sticks that I prefer. For very small eye pupils I use wires mounted in wooden handles. It will help if the wire is roughened slightly by 320 grit metalite cloth. In practice the iris is painted first and allowed to dry. The pupil is then added. When dry, the head and eyes are covered with polyurethane varnish.

Any holes or imperfections in the cork or balsa bodies should be filled and sanded smooth. I use model airplane enamel or acrylic enamels to obtain a smooth surface on the bodies. If the bodies are not smooth, the eyes will run and be oddly shaped. On streamers, the heads should be coated with head cement or varnish so that tying threads are not visible above the surface. Otherwise, the painted eye will run down the thread to form a streak instead of a nice round eye.

For the eyes I use regular oil based enamels or acrylic enamel. The paint is stirred with a small flat stick such as a small tongue depressor or craft stick. (I save the sticks from ice cream bars.) Let the paint stirrer drain to a uniform layer of paint on the stick. Lay the paint coated stirrer on a card. This will provide a paint layer of the proper thickness for the eyes. Take the eye paint stick and touch the layer of paint on the stirrer. Then touch the paint stick where you wish the eye to be. If you get it in the wrong place, simply wipe it off with a cloth. You will be surprised how many eyes can be painted in a few minutes. Do the same for the pupil of the eye.

These paint sticks are useful for putting spots on the ferrules and fly rod sections so that the guides will be lined up properly when the rod is put together.

When coated with a thin layer of varnish, painted eyes are very durable. I have painted thousands of them and have flies that are 35 to 40 years old, and after hard use the eyes are still good.

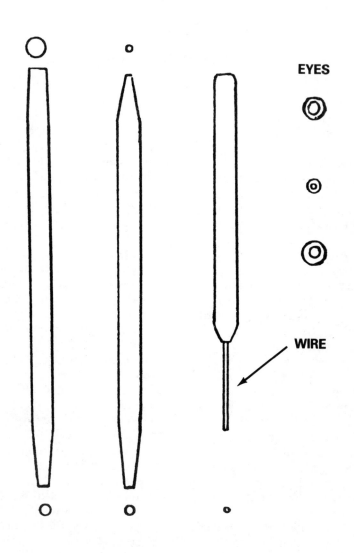

EYES

WIRE

PAINT STICKS

"DOLL EYES" OR "MOVING EYES"

These eyes may be found in craft stores or in the craft section of many department stores. They are made in Japan and distributed by Western Trimming Corporation, Chatsworth, California. They come in sizes from 3 mm (1/8″) to 30 mm (1-3/16″). A clear plastic dome is apparently heat sealed to a base with a ball or flat disc in the sealed space. See sketch. The base is usually white or yellow for the iris of the eye. Other colors of reflective gold and red may soon be available. In the small sizes, up to 4 mm, the pupil is a small plastic ball. In larger sizes the pupil is a disc and is normally black. The pupil of the eye is free to move. They also make owl, cat and frog eyes and I have seen some that wink as the eye is moved.

These eyes can be cemented to a wide variety of fly designs. Silicone rubber cement or "Sportsman's Goop" (Eclectic Products Inc., San Pedro, California 90731) may be used. Goop is useful for repairing wet suits, waders, boots, shoes, etc. Duco cement can be used on cork or balsawood surfaces. When the deer hair head of a bass bug has been trimmed to shape, depressions or sockets (the diameter of the eyes) can be trimmed where the eyes are to go. Place a wad of the Goop in the sockets and press and rotate the eyes to distribute the cement. It is best that the eyes are set into the head. There are reports that some eyes leak and can be broken off. When set in a depression, they are protected.

No doubt, there will be further developments in these eyes.

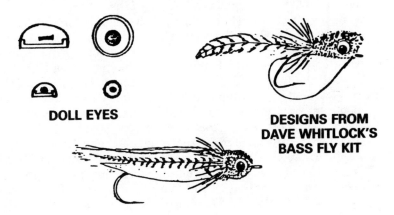

DOLL EYES

**DESIGNS FROM
DAVE WHITLOCK'S
BASS FLY KIT**

A METHOD FOR
SOFT HACKLE FLIES

In some situations soft hackle flies are very effective. They are tied with sparse hackle that wiggles with a tantalizing motion in the current. Most good soft hackle feathers are not suited to winding in the conventional dry fly or wet fly method. The feathers are short and oval in shape with long webby soft barbules. Several methods have been devised to use these valuable feathers. The method to be described was suggested to me by Art Wilson. I have worked with this method for some time. I have used at least a dozen different kinds of feathers as well as rabbit and squirrel hair. Useful feathers are grizzly body feathers, guinea speckled feathers, teal and widgeon side feathers, partridge, grouse, pheasant, hen hackle, grackle and starling. I have since found a somewhat similar method for hair hackles in Lawrie's *All-Fur Flies and How to Dress Them* and in Herter's *Professional Fly Tying Manual.*

The method that I now use is shown in the accompanying 14 sketches:

1. As shown in the first sketch, attach thread to center of the hook and wind forward, leaving the hook bare behind eye. This makes spinning hackle fibers easier.

2. Take the selected feather and arrange about 3/8 " to 1/2 " of fibers so that tips are even and separated from the other fibers of the feather. With your right hand, strip off these fibers.

3. As shown in the fourth sketch, lay fibers on top of the hook with tips pointing out over the front of the hook eye. Adjust to proper length of hackle desired. Hold butts of fibers on top of the hook with your left hand. Take one loose turn and then a tight one around the fibers and allow them to spin to the bottom of the hook so that the bottom half of the hook is covered. If they do not spin, simply push the fibers below and arrange symmetrically around the bottom half of the hook.

4. Add another bunch of fibers to the top half of hook, as shown in the sixth sketch, and take a few turns of thread to the rear. Note: You will now have a hollow cone of hackle fibers extending out over the eye of the hook. Tails if needed and any body type may be formed—dubbed fur, chenille or floss.

5. Trim off excess butts of hackle fibers, as shown in sketch 7.

6. Wind thread to rear and attach rib of size 00 nylon thread the

same color as the floss that will be used, as shown in the eighth sketch. Wind thread forward and attach floss.

7. Wind and rib body, as illustrated by sketch 9.
8. Wind a small ball of dubbed fur between body and hackle, as indicated by the tenth sketch. This is to prevent hackle from laying tight against body when the hackles get wet. The fibers are held away from the body so they can wiggle and move in the current.
9. As shown in sketch 11, you should next insert a tube with an inside dimension that will fit over the eye of the hook into the center of the hollow hackle cone.
10. Push tube straight back to move the hackles in a concentric pattern back over the hook eye, as shown in sketch 12. Grasp feather fibers with your left hand.
11. Wind a few turns of thread to hold the hackle upright as shown in sketch 13, or turn the tips of hackle to the rear for a conventional soft hackle pattern.
12. Wind a small head, whip finish, cut off thread and apply cement to head. You now have the finished fly, as shown in sketch 14.

This is much easier to do than to describe. It opens many avenues, uses materials that might otherwise be thrown away, and produces excellent flies.

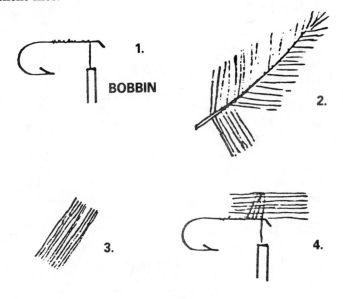

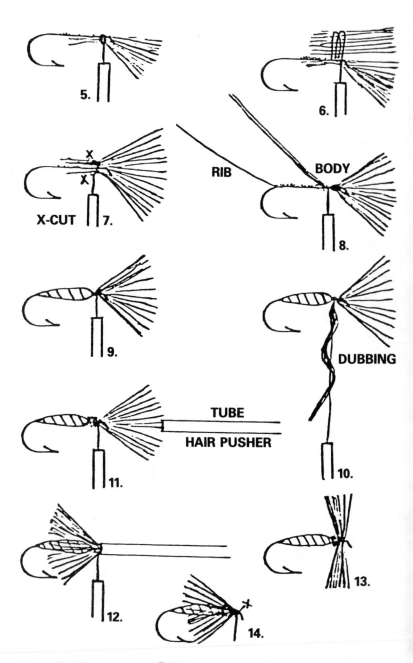

5.

6.

X-CUT 7.

RIB BODY 8.

9.

DUBBING

TUBE
HAIR PUSHER

11.

10.

12.

13.

14.

ANOTHER METHOD FOR
SOFT HACKLE FLIES

Five hundred years ago, Dame Juliana described a partridge and yellow soft hackle fly that is very effective today, especially fishing in a gentle water current. The gray and brown feathers from the Hungarian partridge are beautifully marked and make speckled and wiggly legs on nymphs and excellent hackle for soft hackled flies. Unfortunately there are very few feathers on the bird that are small enough to be wound in the conventional way. The feathers are usually tied in by the the tip and very carefully wound because they are easily broken. In the method to be described, larger feathers can be used for small flies and the flies are very strong and durable. The feathers are spun on the hook somewhat like deer hair is spun when making deer hair bodies.

Hook: Mustad 3906B size 12-14.
Tail: None.
Body: Yellow, orange or green floss.
Rib: Tying thread of the same color as floss.
Dubbing: Tan rabbit.
Hackle: Partridge, grouse, pheasant rump feathers, starling, and the shoulder feathers from the wings of many birds such as coot, crow, and hen pheasant.

Details of the method are shown in 12 sketches:

1. Typical shape of partridge feather is shown in the first sketch.
2. The soft down and some of the hackle fibers are stripped from the base of the feather as shown in sketch 2.
3. Spread the hackle fibers to separate the center rib of the tip and its attached fibers. Clip a length of the rib equal to the length of hackle that is desired on the finished fly. See sketch 3.
4. Prepared feather is shown in the fourth sketch.
5. Wind tying thread over about a 3-inch length of the thread that extends to the rear, as shown in the fifth sketch. This thread will be used to rib the floss body in a direction opposite to that used when winding the floss. This will prevent the floss from sliding to the rear and will greatly increase the durability of the fly.
6. Wind tying thread forward and attach floss, as shown in the sixth sketch. Moisten the floss to remove static charges and prevent fuzziness.

7. Wind floss clockwise to rear and return to produce a fairly thin tapered body. Tie off floss and wind rib in counter-clockwise direction. See sketch 7.
8. Attach fur dubbing and wind a small ball of fur. This holds the hackle fibers away from the body of the fly, as shown in the eighth sketch.
9. Lay prepared feather on top of the hook so that the point of the V is about even with the eye of the hook, as shown in the ninth sketch. This prevents the inclusion of the center stem of the feather when the hackle has been formed. With the left hand push the V together and hold feather flat on top. Take one loose turn with tying thread around the feather and then another turn. Tighten the thread as the left hand releases the feather. The hackle fibers will spin around the hook to form a symmetrical collar of fibers pointed to the rear of the fly.
10. Take two or three more tight turns and clip off the stem and fibers at the front, as shown in sketch 11.
11. Wind a small head and apply cement, as in sketch 12.

This makes nice durable flies. I have tied several hundred flies this way and I have caught a lot of fish with them when conditions are right.

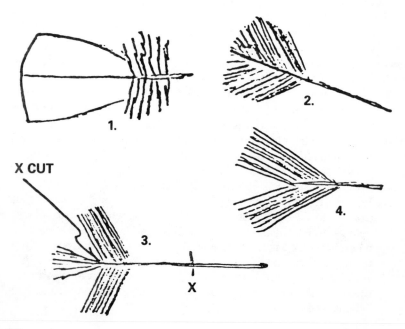

1.

2.

X CUT

3.

X

4.

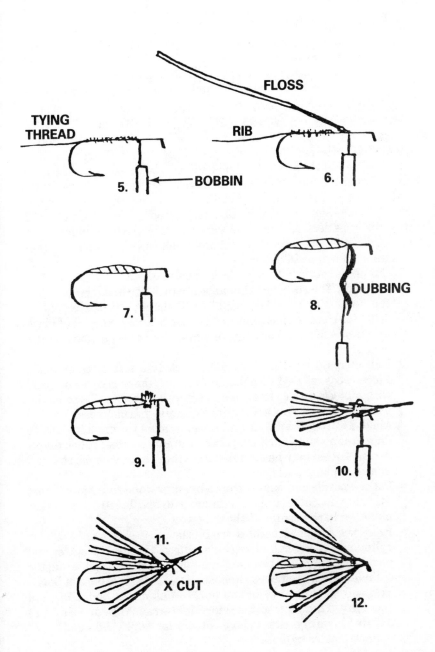

TYING
THREAD

FLOSS

RIB

5. ←BOBBIN

6.

7.

8. DUBBING

9.

10.

11.
X CUT

12.

McMURRAY ANT

Earlier I described Hard Bodied Ants. The McMurray Ant is made with an abdomen (gaster) and head of small cylinders of balsa wood. The head and abdomen are connected with nylon monofilament that serves as the waist or pedicel of the ant. The connecting nylon is tied to the top of the hook and two to three turns of hackle wound over the nylon. These ants have received rave notices in fly fishing magazines. I have given some to fishermen who report results with them that are fantastically good. In the method that I use, the cylinders are cut from various thicknesses of balsa wood cross sections with a sharpened tube similar to a cork borer. The procedure is shown in 13 sketches:

1. Cut cross sections from a block of balsa about 1-1/2″ x 1-1/2″ on the sides. The abdomen should be about 1-1/2 times the length of the head. For cylinders 3/32″ in diameter, lengths would be 3/16″ for the abdomen and 1/8″ for the head. Sand ends of block to remove fuzz and any unevenness. Cut cross sections a little over size.

2. Nail strips 3/16″ thick and 1/8″ thick to a flat piece of wood. Place cross section of balsa in between these strips and sand with a block sander to even and smooth surfaces. These guides make it easier to obtain sections of uniform thickness.

3. Make a cutter from thin wall brass or steel tubing 3/32″ inside diameter as shown. Brass tubes or stainless steel tubes (hypodermic tubes) may be obtained from most hobby shops that sell model airplane parts.

4. Make a needle and pusher from a brass or wood rod that will just fit inside the cutter tube. The number 10 needle (.018″) should be mounted in the center of the push rod.

5. Press the cutter straight down on the cross section of balsa. A cylinder is easily cut. Place the needle rod inside the cutter and push needle through center of cylinder. Continue to push and the cylinder will be removed. Repeat with other thickness of balsa. You will then have cylinders 3/32″ in diameter and 3/16″ and 1/8″ long. These are suitable for McMurray Ants on size 12-14 94840 Mustad hooks. I have cutters for 3/32″, 1/8″ and 5/32″ diameter balsa cylinders.

6. Use Maxima chameleon nylon 10-12 lbs. on .014″ to form a ball

on one end by holding near flame.

7. Make a spacer to keep balsa abdomen and head the proper distance apart. Slots for the nylon are cut in the ends of a 3" long piece of wood 5/16" wide and 3/16" thick.
8. String one 3/16" long and one 1/8" long balsa piece on the beaded nylon.
9. Place assembly in slot of spacer so that the wood pieces are on each side of the spacer. Hold the straight end of the nylon near flame to form a ball adjacent to the end of the balsa wood cylinder.
10. Finish unpainted assembly.
11. Dip each end, one at a time, in paint. Allow to drain and place in a rack to dry. I use small bottles of Testor's model airplane enamel, black for black ants and dark brownish red for red ants. I mix brown with red to get the proper shade for red ants.
12. Tie nylon firmly to hook as shown and apply cement.
13. Wind two turns of hackle as shown.

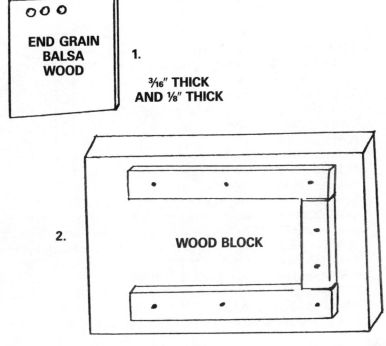

END GRAIN
BALSA
WOOD

1.

3/16" THICK
AND 1/8" THICK

2.

WOOD BLOCK

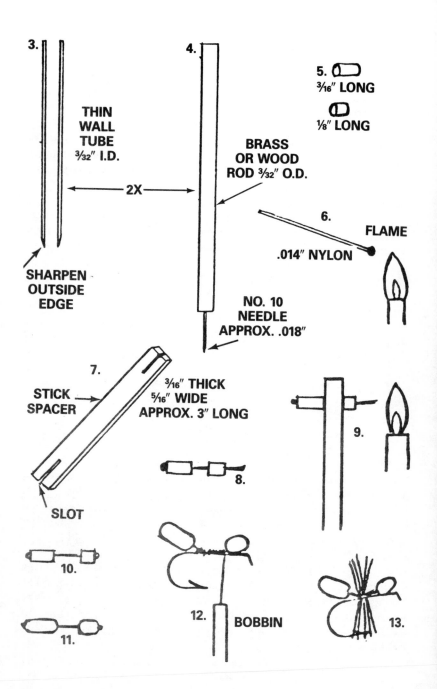

3. THIN WALL TUBE 3/32″ I.D.

2X

SHARPEN OUTSIDE EDGE

4. BRASS OR WOOD ROD 3/32″ O.D.

NO. 10 NEEDLE APPROX. .018″

5. 3/16″ LONG

1/8″ LONG

6. FLAME

.014″ NYLON

7. STICK SPACER

3/16″ THICK 5/16″ WIDE APPROX. 3″ LONG

SLOT

8.

9.

10.

11.

12. BOBBIN

13.

STRAIGHTENING NYLON MONOFILAMENT FOR FLY TYING

Monofilament nylon has a good memory. That means the material, as received in a coil or on a spool, will remain curled when removed from the spool. Hard type nylon (Mason's and others) is difficult to straighten with the hands. Fishing leaders are straightened by pulling the leader through the fingers and holding the leader straight for a few seconds. The nylon is not really straight after this treatment. Absorption of up to 8 percent water will help to soften and straighten the leader. For a number of uses it is desirable to have really straight pieces of nylon. This can be accomplished with a plywood or aluminum plate as shown in sketch 1. Notches are cut with a hacksaw and smoothed with a small file. The nylon is firmly wound through the notches and on both sides of the plate. Place the wound nylon in an oven at about 300° F for a few minutes. I place the plate on an aluminum pie pan so that the nylon does not touch any part of the oven rack. When the nylon has been held at this temperature for about five minutes, it is removed and allowed to cool. When cool, the strands are cut at the notches. You will have perfectly straight pieces of nylon. If the nylon melts, your oven is too hot. Check your oven thermometer and lower the temperature a little.

A non-scratching bobbin threader can be made as shown in sketch 2. For my bobbins, which have a .055″ hole, I use 0.015″ hard nylon. These threaders are quite flexible and will follow curves in any type bobbin. The sleeve is a small tube. I use the brass sleeves sold to make wire leaders. My tubes are Berkley size B2 (.040″), inside dimension. Any small tube will do. Bend the straightened nylon in the middle. Insert the bent end only in the tube opening and place in the oven at 300° F for five minutes. When cool remove the nylon from the tube. There will be a permanent crimp in the bent end that makes it easier to insert in the bobbin tube. Cement the straight ends in the tube with Pliobond or epoxy cement. For other bobbins, different size nylon may be required. I have made hundreds of these gadgets and they work well. In the beginning I used solid stainless steel leader wire or steel guitar strings but I like the nylon better.

Item 3: Wax remover for the bobbin tube. For my bent bobbins I

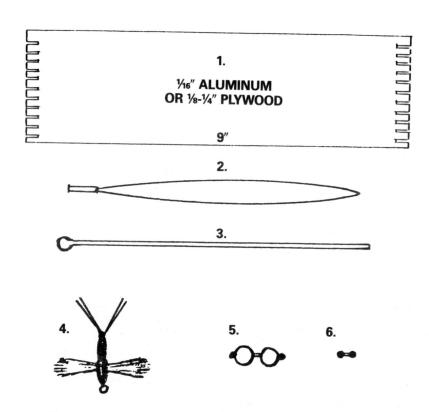

1.

**¹⁄₁₆″ ALUMINUM
OR ⅛-¼″ PLYWOOD**

9″

2.

3.

4.   5.   6.

use .053″ ocean salmon nylon monofilament. A ball is formed on one end of the straight nylon by holding the end near a small flame. Other large size nylon may be found in nylon guitar strings, badminton or racketball strings.

Item 4: Small straight "Maxima Chameleon" leader material makes good outrigger tails for spent wing flies. These tails keep the fly floating on an even keel in fairly fast water.

Items 5 & 6: Straight nylon is much easier to work with when making bead eyes or ball eyes.

Straight nylon is much better for stringing balsa wood sections when making McMurray Ants.

A whip finisher can be made by winding a loop of nylon monofilament on a needle with fly tying thread. In use the nylon loop is wound over by several turns of tying thread. The end of the tying thread is inserted in the nylon loop and pulled through, under the windings, by pulling on the needle. When time is short, these whip finishers are nice for teaching beginners.

WATER PIPE HAIR STACKER

What is a hair stacker? It is a device for evening the pointed ends of hair such as deer hair, squirrel tails or hair, elk hair, etc. It is usually a tube closed on one end. A clump of hair is placed in the tube with pointed ends down. The tube is tapped on a hard surface to bounce the hair. This causes the hair to become even on the bottom or pointed end.

Copper streamline water pipe makes a good hair evener because it is a good conductor and does not build up static electric charges that cause the hair to stick together. Copper pipe is heavy and can bounce the hair with more authority and vigor. It is best if the cap is tall enough to hold the hair erect, without falling over, when the tube is removed from the cap. The cap should be short enough so that the hair can be picked up with the fingers. Very short hair may require a short cap. Excellent hair stackers can be made from copper streamline pipe, caps, and couplings in 1/2", 5/8" and 7/8" outside dimension sizes.

Different hair colors can be blended in the larger size stacker. The colors to be blended are placed in the tube, tips down, and stirred with a stirrer to mix. The stacker is tapped to even the blended hair.

Making these stackers is a good group project. One of my fly tying classes came over to my shop and made a number of the stackers for all of the fly tyers at a cost of a few cents each.

Details for the small stacker are shown in eight sketches:

1. Pipe, cap and coupling can be bought in hardware stores or plumbing shops. Look for caps that fit snugly.
2. Units cut to length.
3.4.5. Wood blocks as thick as the size of the cut piece are convenient. A hole with diameter equal to diameter of the piece is drilled and a thin slot sawed through the center of the hole. The copper piece is placed in the hole and the block clamped in the vise. Cut the piece a little oversize with a hacksaw. File flat and square against the block. Smooth with 320 grit "metalite" abrasive cloth. Remove the burrs and polish with fine steel wool.
6. The longer tube is flared on one end. This can be done with any pointed or tapered tool of the proper size. I have used plumb bobs, the chuck from a hand drill, or even a steel ball. An extra cap is placed on the opposite end of the tube to protect that end. Commercial flaring tools leave ridges on the tube where the tool

clamps the tube. Tube cutters leave edges indented on inside and are not suitable for the intended use.

7. Assemble cap as shown. Regular epoxy cement is completely adequate and easier to use than solder.
8. Short hair in small stacker. For longer hair a larger and longer tube and cap are called for.

Note: These tubes are rarely perfectly round. When the flared tube is inserted in the cap, it can be rotated to find a tight spot so that cap does not fall off. If the fit is too loose, a small drop of solder can be placed on the flared tube where it enters the cap. Rotation will usually find a tight spot. Rotation can then loosen the fit when the tube is to be removed.

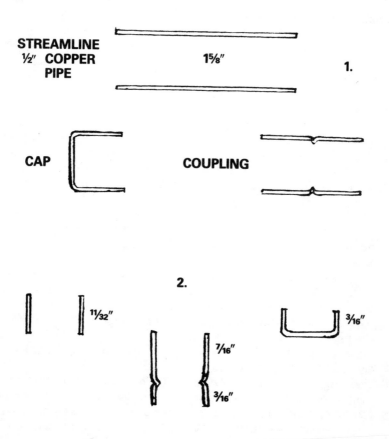

STREAMLINE ½″ COPPER PIPE

1⅝″

1.

CAP

COUPLING

2.

11⁄32″

3⁄16″

7⁄16″

3⁄16″

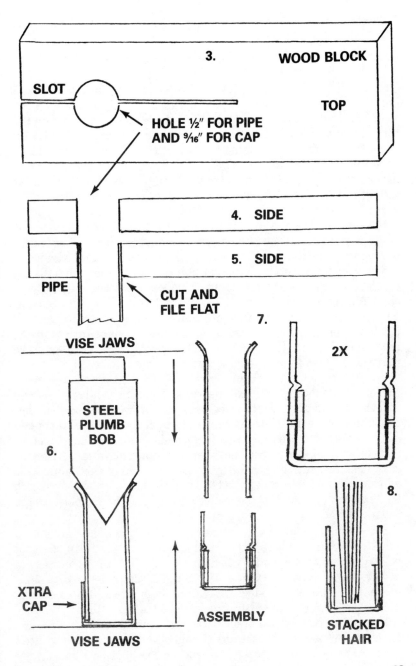

3. WOOD BLOCK

TOP

SLOT

HOLE ½" FOR PIPE
AND 9/16" FOR CAP

4. SIDE

5. SIDE

PIPE

CUT AND
FILE FLAT

VISE JAWS

7.

2X

STEEL
PLUMB
BOB

6.

XTRA
CAP

VISE JAWS

ASSEMBLY

8.

STACKED
HAIR

QUICK NAIL KNOT

One of the best ways to attach a leader to a flyline is with a nail knot or tube knot. About 20 years ago many of us wrapped the leader around a small tube and poked the leader back through the tube and underneath the wraps or winds of leader material—a tricky and laborious task! The method to be described is tied exactly like a hook is snelled. The knot can be tied in about a minute—at home or in the field—even in the middle of the river if necessary. The knot is strong and durable and under normal conditions will last for about a year of fishing.

In order to keep the fly line tip from twisting, a bent wire about .040″ in diameter is used (see figure 1). Hold the wire next to the fly line tip with the fingers of the left hand. Make a loop in the knotless tapered leader with the butt end pointing to the left and the tip extending to the right for about 2 inches. Hold the assembly as shown in figure 1 with the fingers of the left hand. With the right hand grasp the right leg of the big loop and wind tightly toward the left hand for about six turns. After the first wrap or turn is made, cross over this turn (to the left) with the second turn. Then wrap the remaining turns for a total of about six turns.

You will have the situation shown in figure 2. Move the fingers of the left hand forward to grasp the winds. Hold the winds tightly and pull the tip end until all of the leader has been drawn through underneath the wraps. Pull alternately on the butt end and the tippet end of the leader. If necessary, use fingernails to push winds together tightly so there is no space between the adjacent winds. After the knot has been adjusted, pull tightly on each end of the leader. This will shrink the turns and imbed them in the line's finish (see sketch 3). Trim the butt end of the leader and the fly line tip close to the finished knot.

Some people coat the knot with thinned "Pliobond" cement. I have never found this to be necessary. When tied properly, the knot will run through the guides when landing a fish. I think that the use of "Pliobond" hastens the breakup of the fly line's finish because it stiffens the knot to produce more of a hinge effect. This also happens with an epoxy or super glue attached leader.

If you use knotted leaders, tie the butt section to the fly line and then attach the rest of the leader to this butt section. You may use a blood knot or form a loop in the end of the butt section and use interlocking loops with the rest of the leader (see figure 4). Some people attach a butt section with a loop to the line and then attach a new knotless leader with interlocking loops. The butt section attached to the line will be good until the line cracks or the finish on the line tip begins to break up.

I have used this method and knot for 15 years and have not had problems of any kind with it even on heavy fish up to 20 pounds.

QUICK NAIL KNOT

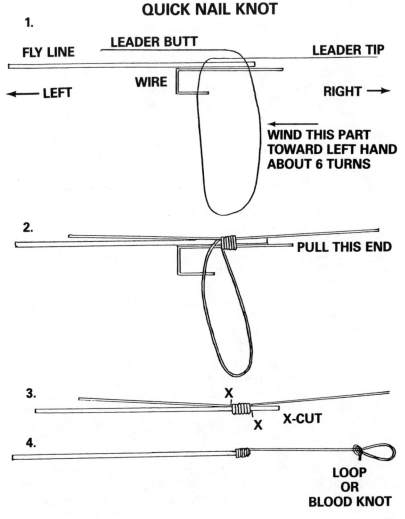

NEEDLE KNOT

I described earlier a nail knot. In a needle knot the leader comes out of the center of the fly line tip. This gives a straighter pull on the line and may make it easier to run through the guides when landing a fish. The needle knot is no more durable than the nail knot but it looks impressive.

In practice a needle is pushed through the center of the fly line and out the side of the line. The butt end of the leader is sliced or shaved to a small diameter with a razor blade. The thinned butt is pushed or pulled through the line's center and out the hole in the side of the line. A nail knot is then tied back from the tip of the line.

I have had some difficulty with hard finished lines, especially sink tip lines. The core of the line appears to be filled with hard material. This makes it more difficult to pass the leader through the line's center. A needle with the point ground off and sharpened to a dome shape will go down the center of the line's core without running out the side until you wish it to.

I have found it easier to sharpen and polish the eye end of the needle to dome shape as shown in figure 1. This can be done on an oil stone in just a few minutes.

The eye of a needle is stamped out before the needle is hardened. The eye end is more or less square and rough. I use several sizes of needles. A practical size is a number 7 "Sharps" (J&P Coats by Milward). This needle measures .027" in diameter with an eye opening that measures .015". The needle is mounted in a wood dowel handle. The needle shown in figure 2 is used to tie the knot. It is a number 1 "Darners" (J&P Coats). It measures .045" in diameter with an eye opening of .025".

In figure 3 the eyed needle is pushed through the center core and out through the side of the line about 3/8 inch from the line tip. The tippet end of a knotless tapered leader is placed in the eye of the needle and the leader pulled through until about 5 inches of the butt of the leader remain outside the side hole in the line as shown in figure 4.

In figure 5 the large needle is placed along the line with the eye just ahead of the side hole in the line and toward the line tip. Wind the butt end of the leader over the needle and line toward the line tip for about five turns. Then insert the end of the leader through the eye of the needle. Move the fingers of the left hand over the winds and pull the needle and leader through and under the winds as shown in figure 6. Move the winds to just cover the side hole in the line and push the winds together so that there is no space between adjacent winds. Pull alternately on each end of the leader to shrink and tighten the winds. Now pull hard on leader ends to imbed winds in the line's finish. Cut off excess leader butt and your knot is finished.

In figure 7 the needle can be inserted as above, removed, and reinserted through the side hole to come out the line tip. The butt of a knotted leader or a short butt section can be sliced or shaved to a small diameter with a razor blade and inserted in the eye of the needle. When the leader is pulled through, the knot is tied as described above.

This whole procedure is much easier to do than to describe! Generally I use this procedure at home and tie the quick nail knot when I am in the field.

NEEDLE KNOT

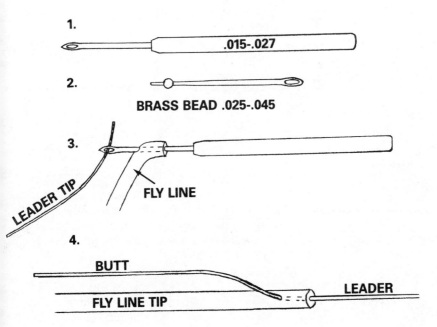

1.

.015-.027

2.

BRASS BEAD .025-.045

3.

LEADER TIP

FLY LINE

4.

BUTT

FLY LINE TIP

LEADER

5.

PULL THRU

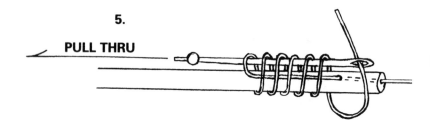

6.

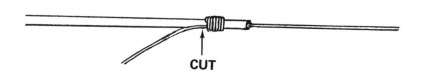

CUT

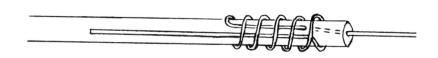

7.

SLICED LEADER BUTT

FLY LINE

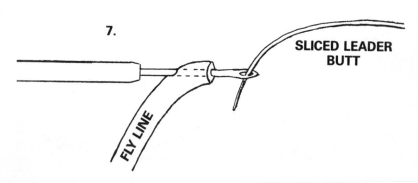

BOTTLES FOR
FLY TYING CEMENTS

The bottle cap sticks so you cannot open the bottle; or you turn the bottle over and spill cement all over your work area. If this has not happened to you already, it will, sooner or later.

For a number of years I struggled with bottle caps that stuck. I would clean the inside of the cap and the threads on the bottle with cement thinner. Nevertheless, once in a while the caps stuck. With much irritation and some swearing I would get a pair of pliers to open the bottle and usually ruin the cap in the process.

In the early 1940's we started using a new fluoride plastic called Teflon for gaskets in chemical reaction vessels. The material is inert and feels slick or oily. Nothing sticks to it. I obtained sheets of various thicknesses and punched out bottle cap liners shown at the left of the photograph. Teflon .010 inch thick worked the best. The liners are placed over the cushioning material in the bottle cap. With Teflon liners I have never had a bottle cap stick. Teflon sheets are available from nearly all plastic distributors or from plumbing suppliers. I now use Teflon sheets and rods of various sizes for many other applications.

I use square medical or hospital specimen bottles. They are about 2-1/2 inches high and 1-3/8 inches on a side. Bottle cap liners 1-1/4 inches in diameter wedge into the caps so that they do not come out. Because of the shape of the bottle it will contain a good volume of cement and because of the low profile it does not readily turn over. To help prevent turnovers, the bottle holders shown can be used. The square ones are made from short pieces of aluminum support posts left over when we added a patio roof over our back porch. The bottles fit snugly. Short cut-off pieces can likely be obtained from builders of patio porch covers. The square aluminum piece is attached to a birch plywood disc 3 inches in diameter and 1/8 inch thick. This produces a very stable cement bottle support that has a low center of gravity. Round cement bottles are usually taller. They can be placed in a wooden block as shown on the right in the photograph.

Various applicator bottles are available. They normally have a rod extending through and above the bottle cap with a needle on the other end of the rod in the cement. In my opinion you are asking for trouble with these applicators because of their height. They are that much easier to bump and turn over. The needle is usually too large for small flies and when removed is coated all over with cement. I prefer to use different sized needles for different sized flies. For instance, a drop of cement on the end of a very small needle is used for small flies.

Some cements are sold with a cone-shaped plastic liner in the bottle cap. When a cement coated cap is placed on the bench, the cement flows down the sides of the cone and comes in contact with the threads of the cap. When the cap is replaced, the cap may be stuck to the threads of the bottle. Something as simple as the Teflon cap liners and bottle holders can save many hours of frustration—not to mention many jars of cement.

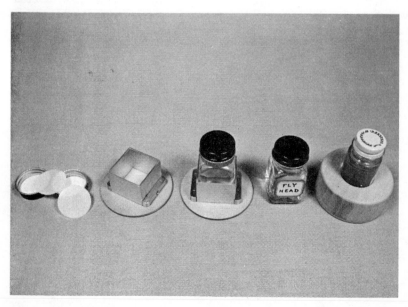

FUR STRIPS FOR FLIES
WITH A LOT OF ACTION

Beer belly rabbit hair "zonkers" as shown in photograph number 1, have been most effective for several years, especially for big fish. It seems likely that this fly evolved from "Matukas" that originated in New Zealand and from the pork rinds that are used by casting and spin fishermen. Rabbit hair matukas, zonkers, wiggle tail nymphs, and rabbit hair bass bugs all have a lot of action in water. They have an even more provocative wiggling action than marabou. For durability and proper action the fur skin should be tanned so that it is soft.

Strips of uniform width can be cut with the cutters shown in photograph number 1. Two to four strips can be cut at a time without cutting the hair. Hardwood spacer pieces are drilled to take 3/48 bolts. These bolts engage the notches in the ends of single edge razor blades. Different widths are obtained by varying the thickness of the spacers.

These cutters are also useful for cutting polyethylene plastic strips used for the backs on shrimp, sowbugs, etc.

The skin can be conveniently held in the device shown in photograph number 2. The skin is clamped with the skin or flesh side up between a wood block and the bracket on the left. The hair (on the underside) should slant to the right. The other end of the hide is clamped between the wood block and the bracket on the right. The skin is stretched by moving the bracket on the right. This bracket is then clamped with the skin taut and smooth. The cutters are moved from the left to right (on skin side). Many uniform strips can be cut in a few minutes without cutting the hair. If you attempt to cut the skins on a flat surface, you will cut most of the hair. After the strips are cut, they are tied in bundles of the same size and color (as shown in photograph number 2) for storage and future use.

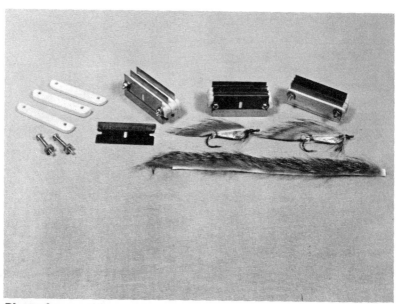

Photo 1

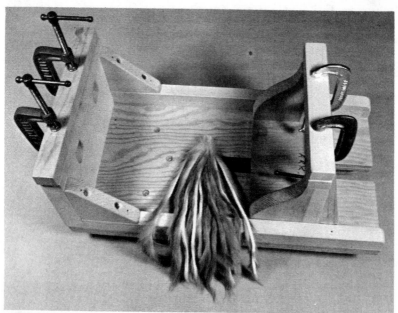

Photo 2

MATCHED FEATHERS
for Streamers, Matukas, Bass Bugs and other Feather Wing Flies

The black ghost and gray ghost flies shown in the photograph usually require at least four feathers of equal length. In most cases two right and two left feathers are used so that the opposing curvatures will produce a more or less straight wing. Matuka wings also require four feathers of equal length and the feather fibers are stripped from the bottom half of the feathers where they contact the body of the fly.

These requirements can be met with the aluminum plates shown in the photograph. In the two on the left, notched rough neoprene rubber sheets are cemented to the plates with pliobond. In use, the proper length of feather is determined and the tip of the feather is placed even with a notch that gives that length. The feather is firmly held against the rubber with the thumb and finger of the left hand while the right hand strips the feather fibers even with the end of the rubber and plate. The center plate will produce nine lengths of feathers.

In the plate at the right of the photograph lines are scribed on the plate. To make it easier on the eyes, the lines are staggered. Gasket rubber is cemented along the end of the plate. To accommodate different feather colors, I use red and black rubber. After determining the proper length of feather, the appropriate line is chosen and marked with an X mark. The tip of the feather is placed even with the selected line and the feather is held on the rubber piece with the thumb and forefinger of the left hand. The right hand strips away the fibers even with the edge of the rubber strip. Many feathers of exactly the same length can be prepared in a few minutes.

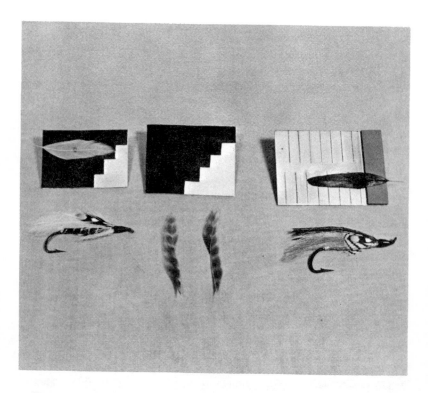

Prepared matuka feathers are shown in the lower center of the photograph. The feathers are stripped to equal length, as described above. The length of the bottom side of the feather that will contact the body of the fly is determined and the proper scribed line on the plate is selected and marked. The tip of the feather is placed at this mark and the fibers on the bottom half of the feather are stripped. Right and left feathers must be stripped on opposite sides so the curvatures will oppose each other and the feathers will fit properly on the fly.

This is a simple device but is extremely helpful when tying matched feather wings of many types.

DUBBING TEASER FOR ROUGHING UP FLY BODIES

In most cases it is desirable for dubbed fly bodies to be loose and fuzzy. This enables the fly to trap air bubbles similar to the way insects do in water and contributes to the translucence that is characteristic of most nymphs. At the same time, the fly must be durable. This can be accomplished by the way the dubbing is wound or the dubbing can be roughed out to form a fuzzy body. For example, by selectively roughing out the dubbing, legs or gills can be simulated where appropriate.

A convenient tool for roughing up dubbing is shown in the photograph. It is made from small "Handy Hack Saw Blades." These blades are from 5-3/4 to 6 inches in length. They are 1/4 inch wide and from .015 to .020 inches thick. They have 32 small teeth to the inch. A number of manufacturers supply these blades: Parker, Nickolson "Little Nick," various English companies, and "Omega" brand. I have used various jig saw blades, coping saw blades, and jewelry blades. The small hack saw blades work best.

The set in the blade is carefully hammered out on a hard flat surface. They are ground as shown so as to get between the hook point and the body of the hook. The blade is smoothed by use of a small oil stone or with "metalite" aluminum oxide cloth, 120 and 320 grit. A 1/4 inch wood dowel is slotted to take the blade. The blade is cemented into the slot with epoxy cement and a thin walled brass tube 1/4 inch, inside diameter, is slipped over the joint and cemented in place with epoxy. These brass tubes are available at nearly all hobby shops.

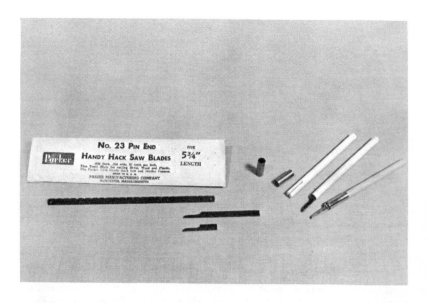

I have used these teasers for many years. They are quite satisfactory on the majority of flies that I tie. For very small flies, 20 and smaller, a broach used by dentists for root canal work can also be used.

MORE ON CARE OF TINSEL

Metallic tinsels are generally more durable than mylar when used in fly patterns that call for tinsels. Metallic tinsels are available in a wide variety of sizes and designs: flat .015 to .045 inch wide, Scotch embossed, English embossed, oval, and solid wire. All come in gold and silver and some are available in colors such as red, green, blue, yellow, pink, and wine. They are available wound on cards or small spools and on larger wooden spools of one ounce or more.

When wound on wooden spools, the end of the tinsel is placed in a slot on the rim of the spool. Because the metal is stiff or springy, it will most likely come loose and produce a bird nest that is difficult to unwind or straighten. If you have experienced this mess you know what I mean. The device shown in the photograph will eliminate this problem. If the hole in the spool of tinsel is rough, fuzzy or out of round, drill a smooth hole with the right size drill. Several slots are cut at the proper angle in the rim of the spool with a jewelry saw. Plastic discs approximately 5/8 inch in diameter and 1/16 inch thick are punched from one gallon plastic milk bottle caps.

A wooden dowel is sanded to just fit the hole of the spool. Because the dowel shrinks and swells with changes in humidity, a slot is cut in the side of the dowel and a spring made from .30 inch stainless steel leader wire is mounted in the slot. This keeps the dowel under constant tension in the hole and makes it easy to push in and out of the spool. The plastic disc is fastened to the end of the dowel with a small screw and washer.

In use, the dowel is pushed up from the bottom so as to leave a space between the plastic disc and the end of the spool. The length of tinsel that is needed is unwound and the tinsel placed in a slot on the rim of the spool and then passed underneath the plastic disc and about half-way around the dowel. The plastic disc is then pressed down against the end of the spool. This will hold the tinsel in place so that it can be handled without fear of the tinsel springing off to become entangled. The tinsel is stored in a screw top bottle. This protects the tinsel from vapors in the air that may cause the tinsel to tarnish or corrode. I have used a number of these for a long time and believe me, they contribute to more relaxed fly tying.

WINDING BOBBINS, SPOOLS, AND SPINNING REEL SPOOLS

Some fly tying bobbins use sewing machine bobbins for holding fly tying threads. They will hold about 100 yards of 6/0 Herb Howard or Fly Master thread. The size of thread can be shown by engraving identifying marks with a sharp instrument near the edges of the side plates of the bobbin. Wooden spools have all but disappeared for fly tying threads. The holes in the plastic spools are often distorted so that they do not run well on most fly tying bobbins.

The metal or plastic bobbins can be wound on a sewing machine or the hand drill shown in the photograph can be used. The gear ratio of 4.5 to 1 will quickly wind a full bobbin. The bobbin is held on a tapered wooden dowel that is mounted in the chuck of the drill. The wooden holder contains a hole for the side handle of the drill. A slot through this hole allows the drill to be clamped firmly in a vise. The chuck end of the drill is pointed upward at an angle of about 40 degrees for easier viewing as the bobbin is wound. I usually wind several bobbins at a time. The extra full bobbins are wrapped in aluminum foil for storage until needed.

I have used this device to wind wire, tinsel, nylon leader material, etc., onto different spools. It works very well for winding spinning line on the spools of spinning wheels. The monofilament is wound without twisting.

IMPROVED ACTION FROM MINI-BLENDERS FOR DRY BLENDING OF DUBBING MATERIALS

Many fly tyers use mini-blenders for mixing fur and yarns for dubbing. These blenders are actually small coffee grinders. The blending action derives from two crossed blades that stir the material. The blending action can be improved by altering the inside volume of the blender.

Dave Whitlock used a thin piece of cardboard glued to a wood dowel. The dowel passed through a hole in the top of the blender. A pumping movement up and down kept the material in contact with the blades. The set up was fragile; and since the cardboard did not fit well to the walls of the blender, some of the material wound up on the top of the paper disc and was not blended to give the proper shade, color, or texture.

Discs were made of thin 1/64 inch plywood and aluminum. Since the inside cavity of the blender was not perfectly round and tapered from top to bottom, the materials used for blending still wound up on top of these discs.

Polyethylene discs were then made from the plastic tops of Cool Whip containers, tops of coffee cans, or tobacco cans. These discs were cut slightly oversize with sharp pointed dividers. The discs are shown at the left of the photograph. Because these discs were flexible, they fit snugly to the walls of the blender. A 3/16 inch brass or aluminum rod was threaded to take the threaded part of post type paper binders. The paper binder was inserted in the center of two wooden discs approximately 1 inch in diameter. These discs are shown in the left of the photograph. The plastic disc is fastened between the wooden discs with three screws. This supports and reinforces the plastic disc. The threaded rod is inserted in the binder post. The rod passes through a 3/16 inch hole drilled in the dome of the blender. Other models were made where the wooden discs were glued to a wooden dowel. The advantage of the metal rod is that the rod can be removed for traveling with the blender. A neoprene rubber tube placed on the rod can be used as a convenient stop for the assembly.

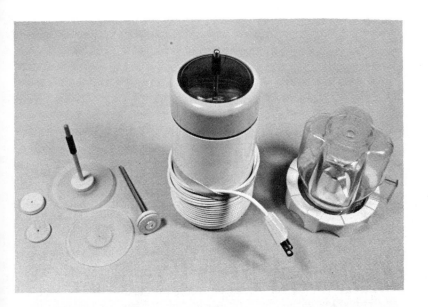

In use, the material to be blended is placed in the mini-blender. The cap of the blender, containing the rod and disc, is put in place and rotated to start the motor. By adjusting the position of the rod, efficient blending is obtained. Aunt Lydia's "Kodel" rug yarn is a difficult material to blend, but is accomplished very quickly with this unit. About 30 seconds time is plenty to give good fiber separation and blending. Longer times simply produce knots. Without the adjusted volume, the fibers are blown up and away from the blades and do not mix very well. This modification has worked well for many kinds of dubbing materials.

The set up at the right of the photograph shows an extra cutter head and baby food jar for a conventional Waring type of kitchen blender.

HOOK SIZE

When different sized hooks get mixed up they can be sorted for size. If you know the model number, such as Mustad 94840 or 3906, the discs shown on the right and left of the photograph can be used. The bend of the hook is placed over the pen in the center and rotated until the rear of the hook eye is even with the perpendicular mark. The size is then readily determined by reading the numbers on the disc.

If you do not know the model number or whether the hook is 1x or 2x long, etc., you may use the device shown in the center of the photograph. This measures the gap of the hook, which is the distance from the point of the hook to the shank of the hook. A set-screw holds the hook straight up and down and places the point of the hook on a ruler graduated in 1/32 or 1/64 inches. A magnifying glass is helpful in reading the fine graduations on the ruler.

Measurements for a number of Mustad hooks (264) are shown in the table. Hook points fall exactly on a 1/32 or 1/64 inch mark on the ruler. There are slight differences for round bend, sproat, and limerick hooks. A fly tyer should have no difficulty in separating hooks according to bend shape. Gaps are the same for long or short hooks. Measurements of lengths as related to gap size reveal that standard hooks are 2.65 times the gap of the hook. The factors are 2x long through 8x long are shown in the chart. Factors for short shank hooks such as 1x, 2x, etc. can be determined in the same way.

I find it particularly interesting that gap sizes are so exact, yet they are in inches instead of millimeters.

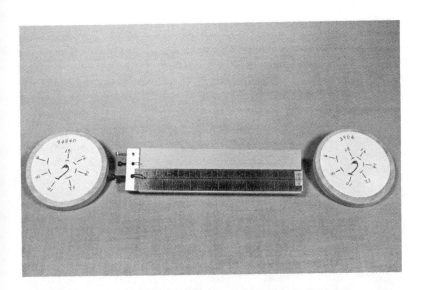

HOOK GAP*

Size	Round Bend (79580, 9672, 9671, 7957B, 94840, 94842)	Sproat (3906, 3906B)	Limerick (3665A, 9575, 36620)
16	4/32″	7/64″	
14	5/32″	9/64″	9/64″
12	6/32″	11/64″	11/64″
10	7/32″	13/64″	13/64″
8	8/32″	15/64″	15/64″
6	9/32″		18/64″
4	10/32″		21/64″
2	12/32″		24/64″
1	14/32″		27/64″

HOOK LENGTH MEASUREMENTS**

Standard: 2.65 X Gap
2X Long: 3.31 X Gap
4X Long: 3.97 X Gap
6X Long: 4.64 X Gap
8X Long: 5.30 X Gap

*Gap is same for short or long hooks.
**Lengths from where eye is formed to far side of bend.

LEADER TIPPET KEEPER
ON FLY REELS

It is most convenient if the leader tippet is fastened to the reel spool. This makes it easier to change spools and to carry extra spools without the leader getting tangled in other gear. Most convenient of all, the tippet end can be easily found instead of becoming buried or wound down into the fly line so that it may cross over itself or the line when pulled off the reel to string up the fly rod.

Some fishermen use velcro fasteners. These have not been satisfactory for me because the leader pulled through the closed velcro fastener too easily.

Instead I have equipped all of my reels with small neoprene rubber washers. The tippet is passed through one of the ventilating holes in the outside plate of the spool and then wound underneath the rubber washer. This system worked very well for a long time.

A wood block that just fits the inside width of the reel spool is forced between the spool side plates. A number 47 drill is used to drill a hole located away from the spool handle and between the ventilating holes. Threads are cut with a 3/48 tap. Any sharp burrs are carefully removed. A 3/8-inch washer is punched from rough neoprene rubber approximately 1/16-inch thick. Punch out a center hole to take a short brass 3/48 round head machine screw. A small thin brass washer supports the central part of the rubber washer. When assembled the screw should be tightened to flare the rubber slightly so that it is easy to pass the leader tippet underneath the rubber washer. The screw should not protrude through to the inside of the reel side plate. Lock-Tite cement is placed on the threads before assembly to keep the screw from turning or loosening.

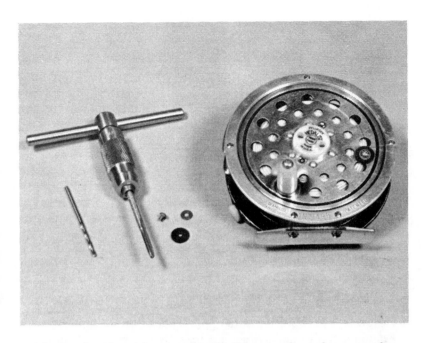

I have a bottle with a supply of rubber washers, brass washers, and screws of the right length. When I get a new reel spool, I can install the washer in about ten minutes.

This little thing makes it easy to string up your fly rod—you can think about fishing instead of a tangled leader and line!

TABLE CLAMP FOR
FLY TYING VISES

As I have traveled to different places for fly tying demonstrations or classes, I have found that the long folding tables used in many schools, churches, and other places have inadequate overhang of table top for clamp-type fly tying vises. The overhang may be 3/8 of an inch. In resort or park areas the table tops may be made of 2 x 4's or 2 x 6's and are 1-1/2 inch thick. Many fly tying vises have clamps that will not open far enough for use on 2 x 4's. These clamps cannot be firmly attached to tables with very narrow top overhangs.

One answer is to carry a large board with a cleat on the bottom that fits against the table edge. But this can be inconvenient and cumbersome.

The clamps in the photograph can be helpful. At the left, 5/8 inch thick hardwood blocks are cut with a wider part at the back and with a cleat on the bottom. The wider part is placed on the table with the cleat against the table edge. Regular C clamps are modified by removing the bars used to turn the screw part of the clamp. Short flat end pieces of the bar about 1 inch long are used to tighten the clamp. These bars are stored in a hole under a brass retaining plate and thumb screw. The clamp end containing the screw and the receiving end of the clamp are ground close to the screw. This allows the clamps to be used on a narrow ledge or tables with very little overhang. The clamps hold the boards with the smaller end protruding. The fly tying vise is clamped on this protruding part.

The clamps shown on the right of the photograph are self-contained with the clamping arrangement as part of the device. They are made from 5/8 inch thick hard maple. The screws are 2-1/4 inch socket head, 1/4 inch cap screws. They are tightened with a shortened regular allen wrench that is about 1/2 inch on one end and 1 inch on the other. These wrenches are stored in a hole in the back end of the wood clamp and retained by a brass plate and thumb screw. The clamp screws work through threaded 1/2 x 1/2 inch cold rolled steel bars. The threads are cut close to the end of the bar so that they will clamp on a narrow table top overhang. Maple blocks 1 inch thick, 1-3/4 inches long, and about 1-3/4 inches high are placed between the top piece and the steel bars. The steel bars are fastened to the top piece through the maple blocks with 1/4 inch bolts that are

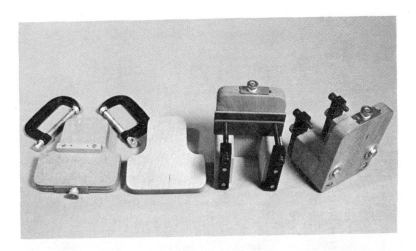

screwed into threaded holes in the steel bars. This makes a very sturdy clamp. Earlier attempts with glue and wood screws pulled apart with the high clamping pressures.

In use, the flat top part is placed on a table top, a piece of "pap-preg," "consoweld," or "mi carta" is placed between the underside of the table and the cap screw ends. The clamps are tightened and the fly tying vise attached with the clamp placed between the two maple blocks on the bottom of the clamp. These clamps are firmly held on table tops with 3/8 inch overhang and on picnic tables up to 1-5/8 inch thick.

After using these clamps I found that I liked them because they moved the vise toward me, away from the table. This makes for comfortable vision because you look down instead of horizontally across the table. Looking across the table when the vise is fastened to the table in the regular way causes strains in neck muscles. I have shortened the support rods on all of my vises and use the maple clamp for all of my fly tying.

LOADING FLY REELS
WITHOUT HELP FROM OTHERS

For many years when I wanted to wind a fly line or backing onto a reel, I had to find someone to put a pencil through the hole in the line container and hold it while I wound the line on the reel. Sometimes I could not find anyone to help.

The device shown in the photograph enables you to wind a new line without the help from others. It consists of a hardwood base about 3 inches wide by 4 inches long and 1 inch thick with a block that extends about 2-1/2 inches above the top of the base. A 5/16 inch round metal rod is fastened to the block. Two shaft collars containing set screws are placed on the rod. Spacers are made from wood thread spools that are cut in half. For maintaining tension 1/8 inch thick soft rubber washers and teflon washers are used.

The base is clamped to the bench with a C clamp. The spool of backing or plastic fly line container is slipped onto the rod. Spacers, rubber washers, and teflon washers are placed on either side of the spool. The shaft collar is pushed snugly against the assembly and the set screw is tightened. The reel is held in the hand while the line is wound smoothly on the reel without twist and with the proper tension.

GOOD USE FOR ROD REEL SEAT

Sporting goods stores often have broken rods that are to be discarded. I have obtained several butt sections that contained reel seats from them. I cut the rod with about 3 inches of the butt section ahead of the reel seat. If the rods are graphite or glass they can be used as they are. I also mounted a reel seat on a 3/8 inch round metal rod 3 inches ahead of the reel seat. The rod can be mounted in the clamp on most fly tying vises.

A reel mounted on the reel seat that is held in the clamp, as shown in the photograph, is useful in several ways.

The line can be wound on a plastic fly line container by placing a pencil in the center hole and another in the extra hole on the side of the plastic line container. After the line is wound on the container, the plastic halves of the container can be separated. The line is slipped off and the coiled line is tied with pipe cleaners, twistems, or string for storage.

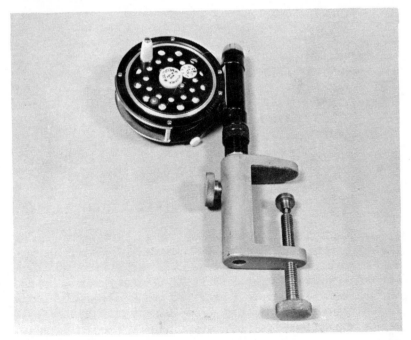

The line is easily transferred to another reel by holding the second reel in the hand and winding the line from the reel in the clamped reel seat. To determine the amount of backing to use, the line can be wound on the reel and then backing on top of the line until the reel is filled to 1/4 or 3/8 inch from the rim of the spool. The backing is then attached to the second reel and wound so that the line is on the outside in the reel spool.

I apply line dressing to the line while the reel is clamped as shown in the photograph. I use Russ Peak's line dressing, which is the slickest dressing that I have ever used. The line is pulled through a small rag saturated with the dressing, then falls to the floor on newspaper. The line is then wound back and forth through a clean rag to remove excess dressing and to polish the line.

This simple device has been useful to me for a long time. I am sure that you can find many uses for it.

DRYING RACKS FOR FLIES

As shown at the top of photograph number 1, alnico magnets are fastened to a hardwood block with brass screws. The top edges of the block are chamfered so that hooks mounted on the magnets will extend beyond the block. Hackles or other parts of the fly will be undisturbed by the block. At the bottom of photograph number 1 plastic magnet strips are fastened to a block similar to the one described above. These plastic strips are 1/2 inch wide and 1/16 inch plus in thickness. They come with contact cement adhesive on the underside. These strips can be obtained at most craft or hobby stores.

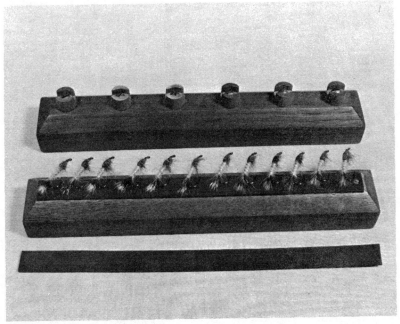

Photo 1

Photo 2

In photograph number 2, flies made on large hooks are mounted in the end grain of a balsa wood block. The end grain will last a long time. Side grain faces will splinter and tear up quickly, especially with hooks having barbs. After considerable use the ends of the block can be dressed to produce a new surface.

Photo 3

In photograph number 3, bead chains are mounted on a wood rack. Hooks can be hung between the beads. This will keep the flies apart until they are dry. Lead head jig hooks can be hung on this rack.

SHARPENING FLY TYING SCISSORS

Good fly tying scissors should be sharp, fine-pointed and thin-bladed in order to make close cuts. Stainless steel scissors must be sharpened frequently. Hard carbon steel scissors are better. Those with tungsten carbide inlays stay sharp the longest.

It is relatively easy to sharpen scissors. A soft pine wood stick as shown in photograph number 1 is helpful. The long piece is about 9 inches long, 5/8 wide, and 7/16 thick. The blocks on the end are 5/8 inch long x 5/8 inch wide x 7/16 inch thick. They are glued and held in place by 1/8 inch wooden dowels. The reason for the wooden dowel is that the top face of the small blocks can be dressed to fresh surfaces for repeated use.

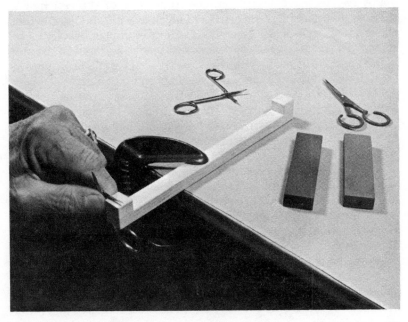

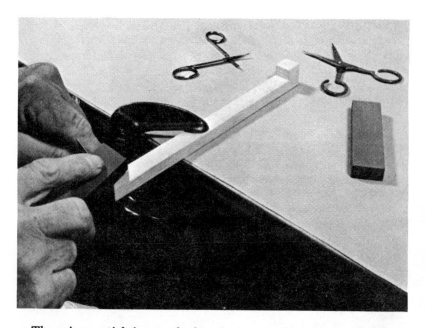

The scissor stick is attached to the bench with a C clamp so that about two inches extend from the front edge of the bench. The scissors are firmly held on the small block at a slight angle so that the original angle of the sharpened face can be approximately maintained. The back edge of the scissors will make a groove in the pine block and can be easily held in place. The elevated surface of the small block allows clearance for the sharpening stone. Good sharpening stones are Norton MB24 and FB24, aluminum oxide stones 4 inches long, 1 inch wide, and 1/2 inch thick. The sharpened edge should be slightly serated instead of smooth like a well sharpened knife or chisel. Scissor blades sharpened with smooth stones, such as hard Arkansas, will let hair slip out from between the two blades. The slightly serated edges will prevent this slippage. The oiled stone is pushed toward and across the scissor blade. Without closing the scissors, sharpen the other blade. Remove the burr on the inside face of the scissor blade with a small hard Arkansas stone. Hold the stone flat against the inside surface of the blade. Make about two strokes down against the burr to cut it off. Close the scissors and try to cut soft facial tissue. If the scissors cut without tearing, check the points to see that they are even. If they are not, grind them even. Dress the outside edges to a fine point. If the blades are too thick, lay the flat surface on the wood block and file or grind to thickness desired. The burr on curved blade scissors can be removed with an oval hard Arkansas stone such as Norton HF853 (this stone is 4 inches long by 1/2 inch wide and is oval in cross section). When closing the scissor blades, the edges should make contact all the way to the tips. Be careful when removing the burr not to remove steel on the inside flat surface at the tip. This will leave a space between the cutting edges at the tip. A good test is to cut through soft tissue and pull on the closed scissors. If they pull away clean, everything is OK. If they pull and tear the tissue at the tip, more work is needed. The blades should overlap each other all the way. The sharp edge should not extend beyond the back of the opposing blade.

Sharpened scissors should be enclosed in a protective scabbard. These can be made from thin leather.

SPLICING LINES
AND LOOPS IN FLY LINES

Many years ago, before weight forward lines were available, we made our own from various lengths of different sized level lines spliced together. They were based on designs developed by tournament distance casters. The ends of the braided lines were frayed for about 1/2 inch by scraping with a dull knife. Two fingers were pushed together in a symmetrical fashion and tightly wound with two layers of thread. The joint was then coated with spar varnish. These lines worked very well.

Before the advent of nail knots and needle knots, loops were spliced in the fly line tip to take the perfection loops of gut or nylon leaders. Today loops may still be used on fly line tips and on shooting heads where they are attached to running lines. Loops on shooting heads make it easy to change heads as the need arises.

The devices shown in the photograph are helpful for splicing lines or loops. They are made from 3/8 inch stainless steel tubes. For holding the line, the ends were flattened and a bolt head brazed through a hole in the flattened part. Large fender washers, soft rubber washers and a wing nut to tighten the washers were added. The soft rubber washers hold the line firmly without damage to the line. The lower end of the tubes were reinforced by tight fitting round rods that were pushed inside the tubes. This reinforcing was where the tubes were to be clamped into regular fly tying vise clamps.

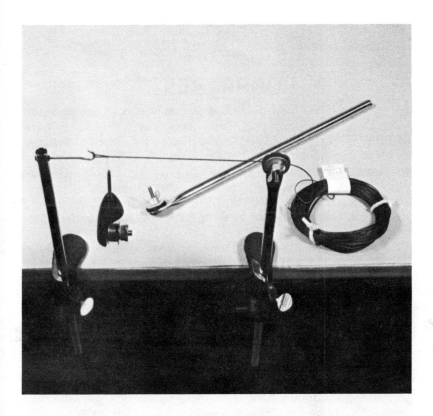

As shown, for loops, a stainless steel hook was brazed to the top end of the bar on the left. About 1/2 inch of the line's finish is removed and 1/2 inch of the line's end is frayed. The loop is formed and placed in the hook. The line is placed between the rubber washers on the rod on the right. Several tight turns of thread from the bobbin are made to the right. The standing part of the line is then stretched tight and straight and held by the rubber washers in the stand at the right. The bobbin is used to wind thread to the right past the end of the frayed line and then wound back over the winds to the left past the starting point. A whip finish completes the loop. The windings are coated with varnish.

BOBBIN RESTS

Over the years I have made and used a number of bobbin rests. For some tying operations a bobbin rest is very useful. They are useful when tying fancy salmon flies where many kinds of feathers and hair may be used in a fly or when tying large streamers and bucktails. In some cases it is desirable to have the bobbin out of the way but close to the fly tying hook. In other situations, where contact cement is applied to the thread, it is helpful for the bobbin to be positioned at some distance from the hook, as is the case when dubbing loops are used.

At the left of photograph number 1, a rest rod supports a cradle where the bobbin may be laid. It is made from 3/16 inch oxweld welding or brazing rod. When heated with a torch this material becomes soft so that it can be tightly wound around a 3/8 inch rod to form a spring-like support for the rod. The cradle is made from 1/16 inch brass and a 1 inch square piece of brass that is attached to the bottom of the cradle. The square piece is threaded to take threads on the end of the support rod. This rest can be positioned where needed

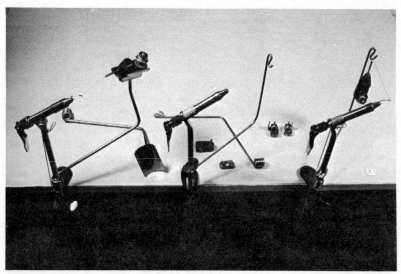

Photo 1

or moved completely out of the way by rotating the rest around the support rod of the vise.

In the middle of photograph number 1, the rest is made from 1/8 inch oxweld. The heated rod is wound around a 3/8 inch rod to form the support for the rest. The thread from the bobbin is placed in a hook bent into the top end of the rest. The position of the rest is controlled by a pen stop that is contained in a brass block that is clamped to the vise support rod. The block contains a 3/8 inch hole and is slotted so that a cap screw can tighten the clamp to position the rest at the desired place.

At the right, a two position stop is used. A brass block clamped on the vise support rod contains a stop pen and a stop that can be moved in or out of contact with the bobbin rest rod. This allows the bobbin to be positioned close to the fly tying hook or at a distance from and at the back of the fly tying vise.

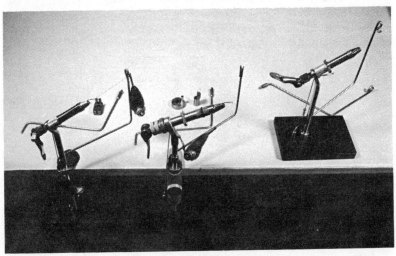

Photo 2

At the left of photograph number 2, a brass clamping block contains two steel tubes, 1/8 inch inside diameter, that function as bearings for the bobbin rest rod. The bottom end of the rest rod is rounded and rotates in the steel bearing which extends about 5/8 inch above the clamping block. The bobbin rest rod can be placed in either steel bearing to obtain a close position to the hook or a longer away spot to the rear of the vise. The thread from the bobbin is placed in a bent hook at the top of the bobbin rest.

In the middle of photograph number 2, a round shaft collar with a clamping capscrew contains a single steel bearing. The straight bottom end of the bobbin rest rod rotates in the steel bearing. A brass sleeve that is cut out of one half of its diameter at the top and is thickened by a block on the other half is placed on the vise support rod. By rotating the sleeve, two positions of the bobbin rest can be obtained. The weight and position of the bobbin will always pull the bobbin rest rod to the stop. The thread from the bobbin is placed in a V-shaped square brass block that is fastened to the top of the bobbin rest rod. If a weighted string that passes through a hole near the top of the vise support is used for modified Thompson type hackle guards, a stainless steel hook attached to the string can be used to hold the bobbin below and to the left of tying operations.

If the fly tying vise is supported on a flat base, holes can be drilled in the base to take the bottom end of the rest at the proper places to give different bobbin positions. A brass sleeve stop is fastened above the bottom end of the rest rod for additional support.

The advantage of straight bottom ends of the rest rods is that the rest can be readily removed if not wanted.

A FLY TYING BOBBIN

When I started tying flies there were no fly tying bobbins. The thread was held in a clip or rubber button mounted on the table edge underneath the fly tying vise. Today few people will dispute the fact that better, tighter, and less bulky flies can be tied with the use of a bobbin. The bobbins to be described have served me well for a long time. I have a separate bobbin for each size and color of thread that I use. I have thoroughly enjoyed improving the design to a point where the bobbins are a real joy to look at and use. Perhaps, if the excellent midge bobbins by Matarelli had been available, these bobbins would not have been made.

At the left of photograph number 1 is a bobbin that I made in the early 1940s. A flat bronze spring was mounted in a slot in the wood underneath the tube. This spring applied tension on the sewing machine bobbin that contained the thread. Tension was adjusted by a brass nut on the bolt that held the bobbin. The tube was hard brass hydraulic tubing that was available at that time.

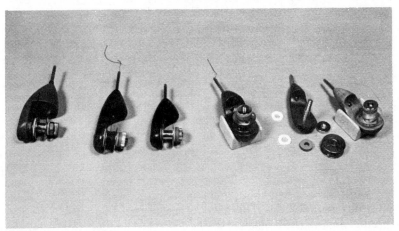

Photo 1

Second from the left is a large symmetrical bobbin with a curved cut out for the screw and the sewing machine bobbin. I used stainless steel tubing and teflon washers for smooth operation. "Scimatco" rubber washers supplied the tension and function to keep the knurled nut from turning.

Third from the left is a smaller version which I made in 1950. Dimensions and specifications for parts may be seen in the drawing. The bobbins worked very well. After several years of hard use the abrasive properties of the nylon thread started to cut a groove in the back end of the tube. This was caused by the thread staying in one place as it entered the rear opening of the tube. This was made worse by the sharp angle of the thread as it entered the tube. No problem has occurred at the front end of the tube because the thread rotates completely around the end of the tube.

Fourth from the left, the hole for the tube was drilled at angles to the left and upward toward the top of the bobbin. The latter angle placed the tube in the center, up and down, of the sewing machine bobbin. The angle to the left allowed the thread to enter the tube straight down the middle of the tube. This occurred when the bobbin was half filled. With a full bobbin the thread touches the left side of the tube hole. With a nearly empty bobbin the thread is on the right side of the tube hole at the rear of the bobbin. When the thread is unwound from the top of the sewing machine bobbin the thread works to the top of the tube opening. When the thread comes from the bottom of the sewing machine bobbin the thread moves to the bottom of the tube hole. In other words, the thread works completely around the rear opening of the tube. This prevents cutting a groove at this point. The tube was bent to fit the angles in the wood part so that a balanced and symmetrical bobbin resulted. The front end of the tube was straight and near the center of the wood part. At this point silicone rubber washers were used for tension because of their excellent durability.

The present model preferred is shown in the two bobbins on the right of the photograph. The tube is straight. The hole in the wood part is drilled straight down the wood but offset to the left and toward the top. The sewing machine bobbin is offset to the right so that the thread enters the rear of the tube at its center. The wood part is skewed at the right. This concave surface makes a good place for the thumb when the bobbin is held in the right hand. Other specifications are similar to the bobbin described above.

The steps in the construction of these bobbins are shown in the following photographs. In photograph number 2, blocks of hard-

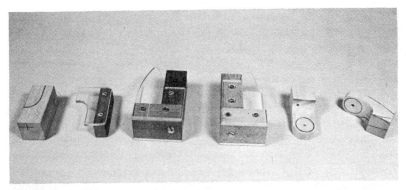

Photo 2

wood, walnut, cherry, rosewood, etc., are cut 1-1/32 inches square and 2-3/8 inches long. Holes for the tube and the stud are drilled while the block is square. The hole for the tube is offset 1/4 inch from the center of the block and 5/32 inch toward the top of the block. The hole for the stud is drilled in the center and 7/16 inch from the rear end of the block. Threads measuring 10/24 are cut in the rear hole for the stud. The block is marked using the Lucite patterns, shown second through fourth from the left. The curved section is cut out with a band saw and the surface smoothed with a fine toothed half round file. The rear of the bobbin is rounded on a disc sander. The block is cut to the pattern lines to form a four-sided block tapering to the tube end of the bobbin.

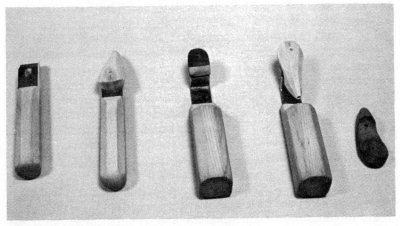

Photo 3

The bobbin blocks are mounted on the eight-sided handles shown at the left of photograph number 3 with washers and 10/24 machine screws. The eight-sided handle permits the four sides to be smoothed on a disc sander. The corners are cut off on the disc sander to produce an equal-sided eight-face piece. The corners of the eight-sided piece are cut off with a half round file. This gives a 16-sided piece. The roughed out block is sanded with decreasing size of grit until 500 to 600 grit sandpaper is reached. The block is then mounted in the handles shown third and fourth from the left in the photograph. The back end is rounded and sanded as above.

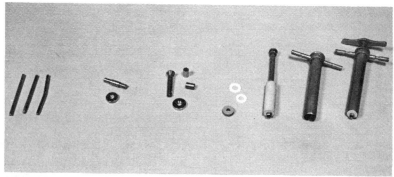

Photo 4

Seamless stainless steel tubes 1/8 inch, outer dimension, and .055 inch, inner dimension, shown at the left of photograph number 4, are cut to length and dressed square on the ends. The front end of the tube is tapered slightly. A smooth shallow radius is formed in the end of the tubes with different sized drills and tapered reamers. If the bores of the tubes are rough, the tubes are strung on 7 cord linen shoemakers thread. The thread is coated with valve grinding compound and the tube pushed back and forth to produce a smooth hole in the tubes. The ends are buffed on a cloth wheel buffer coated with fine abrasive. This produces polished smooth ends with no sharp edges to cut thread. The tubes are washed clean and dried. They are cemented in the tube hole of the wood part with epoxy cement. Brass studs are shown second from the left on the photograph. They are made according to specifications in the drawing except the top end of the stud and knurled nut have 10/32 threads. Nuts and bolts measuring 12/24 are no longer standard and may be hard to find. The knurled nuts are made from 10/32 thumb nuts (battery terminal nuts) by cutting off the lower tapered part.

If studs are not available, flat head brass or stainless steel bolts can be used. The wood part is countersunk so that the bolt head is flush with the wood. The bolts are screwed into the threaded hole in the wood part. If bolts are used, thin-walled brass tube bushings that fit the hole in the sewing machine bobbin can be placed over the threaded part of the bolt. Bolts and bushings are shown third from the left in the photograph.

Washers are cut from 1/8 inch thick soft silicone rubber sheets. Silicone rubber comes in different degrees of hardness and does not oxidize to become hard, brittle, or sticky like gum rubber. These washers are 7/16 inch in diameter with a 0.140 inch hole. The hole must fit tightly on the stud in order to keep the knurled nut from turning, causing the tension adjustment to change. Teflon washers are cut from flat sheets 1/32 inch or 0.030 inch thick. All of the washers are punched out with cork borers that are shown at the right of the photograph. The outer diameter is punched with the larger borer and then the center hole is punched with the smaller size borer. In order to have the small hole in the center of the washer, a dowel bushing that fits the small borer and the inside diameter of the larger borer is used as shown in the photograph.

After the tube has been cemented in the tube hole, the wood is finished with tung oil and bakelite or phenol formaldehyde resin. The wood is polished and waxed with hard paste wax.

The stud is screwed into the threaded hole and a teflon washer placed over the stud next to the wood. The sewing machine bobbin is put in place and a teflon washer added. The silicone rubber washer is screwed into place and the adjusting nut put in place. We now have the finished bobbin as shown in photograph number 1.

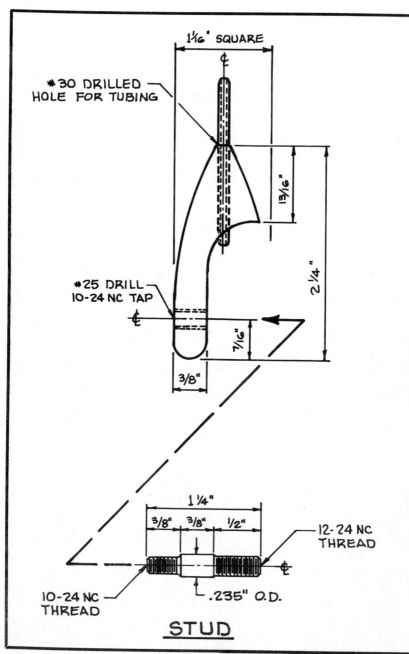

1¹⁄₁₆" SQUARE

#30 DRILLED HOLE FOR TUBING

13⁄16"

2¹⁄₄"

#25 DRILL
10-24 NC TAP

7⁄16"

3/8"

1¼"

3/8" 3/8" 1/2"

12-24 NC THREAD

.235" O.D.

10-24 NC THREAD

STUD

MATERIAL REQUIRED

QTY.	DESCRIPTION
1	SEAMLESS STAINLESS STEEL TUBING, 1/8" O.D. , .055" I.D. , × 1 3/4" LONG
2	TEFLON WASHERS, 1/32" THK. , 7/16" WIDE , 15/64" HOLE
1	"SCIMATCO" RUBBER TUBING 3/16" I.D. × 1/8" WALL × 1/8" LONG
1	KNURLED NUT, 12-24 NC THREAD , 1/2" DIA. × 1/8" THK.
1	SINGER SEWING MACHINE BOBBIN

FLY TYING JIG
SMALL SIZED BOBBIN

SCALE FULL	REVISIONS		BY	DATE
DATE	DESIGNED BY W.E. MOORE - 1950			
DR'N. RDS	CKD.			
AP'VD.				
TITLE		NO.		

FLY OF THE MONTH AND A COMMEMORATIVE FLY

Four dozen flies using this pattern were tied for The Green Country Fly Fishers Club of Bartlesville, Oklahoma. They used the flies for their "Fly of the Month" program. The pattern was modified for the commemorative fly by using light gold dyed grizzly wings and adding a simulated egg sack. This fly represented a recently hatched trout with egg sack still attached. The fly was given to all of the members of the White River fly fishers who took part in the trout egg planting projects. This club has planted more than one million trout eggs in the White and Norfork River systems.

Materials For Fly of the Month:
Hook: Mustag 9672 Size 8
Thread: Nymph, white
Body: White floss, Pearsall's stout silk
Rib: #14 embossed silver tinsel
Eyes: Plastic beads, 3 mm size
Underwing or Beard: Small amount of polar bear hair
Wings: Matched pair of golden badger saddle hackle

Materials for Commemorative Fly:
Wings: Grizzly saddle hackle dyed light gold
Egg Sack: golden yellow Fly-Rite yarn.

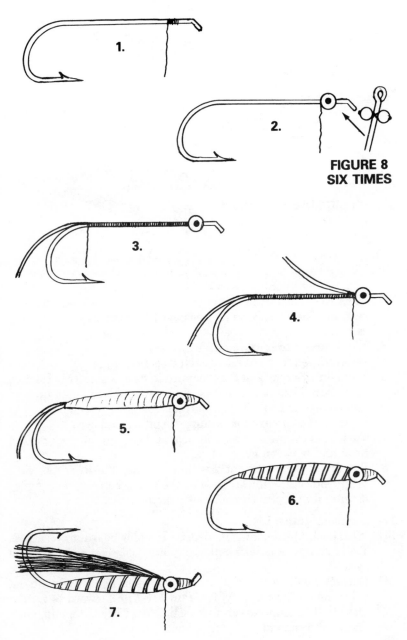

1.

2.

FIGURE 8
SIX TIMES

3.

4.

5.

6.

7.

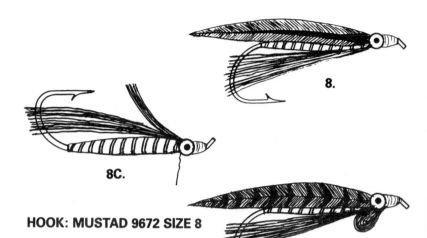

HOOK: MUSTAD 9672 SIZE 8

Tying Instruction:
1. Wrap a small area of the hook shank near the eye with thread and apply cement.
2. Construct bead eyes on nylon monofilament as described in section "The Eyes Have It" (see page 25). Attach eyes and apply cement.
3. Wind thread to rear and attach tinsel.
4. Wind thread forward and attach floss near eyes.
5. Wind floss to rear and then forward to form a smoothly tapered body. Wind floss between eyes (figure 8) and build up a tapered head to eye of hook. Tie off and cement.
6. Wind tinsel forward for ribbing, tie off behind eyes.
7. Turn hook over in vise and tie-in polar bear hair on underside of hook and between eyes.
8. Return hook to upright position in vise. Tie in wings with bright side out. Wind stems of feathers between eyes with figure 8, whip finish, clip thread, and cement.

For Commemorative Fly:
8C. With hook upside down in vise, tie in polar bear hair as above. Tie in strand of golden yellow Fly-Rite between and to rear of eyes.
9C. Replace hook in upright position in vise. Let Fly-Rite hang below hook and tie in wings. Pull Fly-Rite forward to form a loose ball to simulate an egg sack. Tie off Fly-Rite, clip, whip finish, and cement.

Wayne Moore is shown during one of his many fly tying demonstrations, here at the National Conclave of the Federation of Fly Fishers in West Yellowstone, Montana in 1982. Wayne was Chairman of the Fly Tyers.

To order
Wayne Moore's
FLY TYING NOTES:

Wayne Moore's Fly Tying Notes is available from the publisher. Write **Recreation Consultants, P.O. Box 842, Seattle, WA 98111** for ordering information. Dealer inquiries invited.